I
LOVE
OKLAHOMA

JAKE TROTTER

TRIUMPH
BOOKS

Library of Congress Cataloging-in-Publication Data

Trotter, Jake, 1981–
  I love Oklahoma / I hate Texas / Jake Trotter.
    p. cm.
  ISBN 978-1-60078-569-6
  1. Oklahoma Sooners (Football team)—History. 2. University of Oklahoma—Football—History. 3. Texas Longhorns (Football team)—History. 4. University of Texas at Austin—Football History. I. Title.
  GV958.U585T76 2012
  796.332'630976—dc23

                                                                    2012013872

This book is available in quantity at special discounts for your group or organization. For further information, contact:

  Triumph Books LLC
  814 North Franklin Street
  Chicago, Illinois 60610
  (312) 337-0747
  www.triumphbooks.com

Printed in U.S.A.
ISBN: 978-1-60078-569-6
Design and editorial production by Prologue Publishing Services, LLC
Photos courtesy of AP Images unless otherwise indicated

CONTENTS

ACKNOWLEDGMENTS

SPECIAL THANKS TO those who agreed to be interviewed for this book: Anthony Stafford, Barry Switzer, Berry Tramel, Bill Krisher, Billy Brooks, Bob Burris, Bob Warmack, Cale Gundy, Carl Dodd, Carl McAdams, Charlie Mayhue, Claude Arnold, Clendon Thomas, Danny Bradley, Dean Smith, Derrick Strait, Derland Moore, Ed Lisak, Eddie Hinton, Gary Baccus, Greg Sellmyer, Jack Ging, Jakie Sandefer, Jamelle Holieway, James Allen, James Winchester, Jarrail Jackson, Jay Wilkinson, John Brooks, Jimbo Elrod, Joe Fletcher, Joe Rector, Joe Washington, Joe Wylie, John Pellow, John Roush, John Shelley, Jon Cooper, J.D. Runnels, Keenan Clayton, Ken Mendenhall, Lance Rentzel, Leon Crosswhite, Mark Bradley, Mike Brooks, Patrick Collins, Richard Ellis, Rickey Dixon, Roy Williams, Rufus Alexander, Ryan Reynolds, Scott Hill, Steve Davis, Steve Zabel, Teddy Lehman, Thomas Lott, Tinker Owens, Tom Carroll, Tommy Gray, Torrance Marshall, Zac Henderson, and lastly Merle Dinkins, who passed away two weeks after giving his interview.

I also appreciate Berry Tramel, David Bossity, LandThieves.com, Mike Brooks, and the OU Touchdown Club for their help in putting everything together. Lastly, special thanks to all the Oklahoma City–area coffee shops that allowed me to loiter while I worked on the book, my dad for letting me use his office at night, and my wife, Rachel, for putting up with the all-nighters.

INTRODUCTION

TEXAS LEARNED EARLY on what happens when you mess with Oklahoma. In 1931 the two states constructed a free bridge across the Red River from Durant to Denison so their citizens would no longer be forced to use toll bridges. But when private companies in Texas that owned the toll bridges sued the state for damages, Texas Governor Ross Sterling closed the free bridge before consulting his neighbors to the north.

Oklahoma Governor Bill "Alfalfa" Murray, who never feared a fight and sometimes wielded a six-shooter, retaliated by sending the Oklahoma National Guard to take down Sterling's barricades. Sterling threatened to call in the Texas Rangers. But that didn't faze Murray, who had also dispatched a machine gun and howitzer platoon to guard the bridges, "He can dig up the biggest army," Murray said. "But I have got the biggest organized army. All Texas Rangers can do are cuss and shoot craps."

Sterling and the Texas state legislature finally capitulated to Murray, and the bridges were opened for good. It wouldn't be long before Oklahoma began taking it to Texas on the gridiron, too.

Since the Red River Bridge War, the two football programs are close to even in the series. But the Sooners claim more national championships, more conference championships,

more Heisman Trophy winners, more All-Americans, and hold the greatest winning streak in college football history. "What they've done doesn't add up to what we've accomplished— we've been dominant," said Barry Switzer, who lost to Texas just five times in 17 seasons coaching the Sooners. "I guarantee they think more of us than we do of them."

This cuts to the core of the Red River Rivalry. The Longhorns have infinitely more resources, money, and power. And still Texas hasn't been able to buy Oklahoma's success on the field. Longhorns believe they ought to be superior to Oklahoma. And yet, they haven't been.

While preparing this book, I polled more than a hundred OU fans to determine exactly what they hated about the Longhorns. The overwhelming majority responded with the same word: "arrogance." Such arrogance chased proud programs Nebraska and Texas A&M out of the Big 12, which nearly destroyed the conference. Such arrogance provided the Longhorns with the capacity to claim the 2008 Big 12 championship with an asterisk, as if the loss to Texas Tech didn't count and the title game against Missouri wouldn't have mattered. Such arrogance gave Texas the nerve to close down a bridge it didn't build on its own.

This is why Oklahomans love to hate the Longhorns. And why they love beating them even more.

1

GAMES WE LOVE

1971

OKLAHOMA	14	17	7	10	48
TEXAS	14	7	6	0	27

Before the 1970 season even started, Chuck Fairbanks was on the verge of being fired. He knew it. Offensive coordinator Barry Switzer knew it, too. Oklahoma had lost eight games the previous two seasons, and had beaten Texas just once since 1957. In the spring, the Sooners decided to scrap the I formation to compensate for the graduation of Heisman Trophy fullback Steve Owens. Switzer begged Fairbanks to install the wishbone. Instead, Fairbanks put in the Houston veer, an offense Fairbanks was familiar with from his days as an assistant with the Cougars. In Norman, however, the veer proved to be a disaster.

The Sooners slipped by SMU and Wisconsin, but lost to unranked Oregon State at home by two scores. OU gained just 190 yards of offense and got the ball to split end Greg Pruitt just four times. Quarterback Jack Mildren threw for just 87 yards on 20 attempts. "We were an embarrassment," Switzer said. "We couldn't make a first down, and we were so much

quicker and faster than them. We looked inept." Everywhere, "Chuck Chuck" bumper stickers had popped up. Switzer felt it was time to try something desperate. "We were doing the wrong thing," Switzer said. "We had speed. We had Mildren. We had Pruitt and [Joe] Wylie. Great Texas speed. Texas wasn't recruiting the black athlete, and we had 'em." With an open date before Texas, Switzer pitched the wishbone to Fairbanks one more time. "I went in and told Chuck, 'We're going to get our asses fired. They're going to fire your ass, which means we're all gone. You need to make a decision,'" Switzer said. "I figured by this point he was ready to listen to any damn foolish idea I might come up with, including changing our whole offense within a few days of playing our biggest rival."

Fairbanks said he'd sleep on the suggestion, but Switzer wasn't confident he'd go through with it. "I knew he would call all

OKLAHOMA

TOP 5 OU RUSHING GAMES vs. TEXAS

1. **De'Mond Parker** | 291 yards | 1997
   31 carries, 3 TDs | 27–24 (Texas)

2. **Quentin Griffin** | 248 yards | 2002
   32 carries, TD | 35–24 (OU)

3. **Adrian Peterson** | 225 yards | 2004
   32 carries | 12–0 (OU)

4. **Greg Pruitt** | 216 yards | 1971
   20 carries, 3 TDs | 48–27 (OU)

5. **Jerald Moore** | 174 yards | 1995
   21 carries, 2 TDs | 24–24 (tie)

his coaching friends at Michigan State and they'd tell him to stick with what he believed in," Switzer said. "I was kinda depressed about it." But the next morning, Fairbanks agreed to give the wishbone a shot, and that same day, Switzer called a team meeting with the offensive players. "We're not going to practice today," he said. "We're going to put a completely new offense in today." The players, notably Mildren and Wylie, were skeptical. "I was like, 'You just don't do this in the middle of the season,'" Wylie said. "I thought we'd be better off sticking to what we were doing."

Switzer knew better. He explained that the Sooners could continue being mediocre with what they were doing or take a chance at being great. The OU coaches had always marveled at how efficient the wishbone had been for the Longhorns, and how effectively it created numbers mismatches. Because of the speed OU possessed, Switzer believed the Sooners could take the wishbone to another level. "I'm going to coach every position on this team," Switzer told the players. "Every position is going to understand what we're doing across the board."

Over the next 13 days, the offensive backs met an hour before practice and rehearsed the running lanes, exchanges, and pitches of the wishbone option. Switzer taped off the lines on the turf so the players knew where they were supposed to run. "It seemed like we were out there forever following those lines," said fullback Leon Crosswhite. "It was so monotonous—but it would be so worth it."

The next week, the Horns crushed OU 41–9—UT's largest margin of victory in the series since World War II. The fans

were outraged, and the papers slammed Fairbanks for making such a drastic change to his offense in the middle of the season. "Chuck," the *Daily Oklahoman's* Bob Hurt wrote, "you don't surprise Texas playing the wishbone T any more than you surprise Hoagy Carmichael by playing 'Stardust.'"

Switzer, however, came away pumped. The Sooners had made 16 first downs and gained 212 yards on the ground. Turnovers proved to be OU's true undoing. "We were controlling the ball, getting first downs," Switzer said. "I'm saying, 'Shit, we're growing, we're going to get it.'" Not everyone agreed. Assistant Larry Lacewell relayed the message of hope to federal judge Frank Seay, a diehard Sooners fan, who told Lacewell to tell Switzer, "Any more games like that, and he'll be going down I-35."

The following week, however, OU knocked off 13th-ranked Colorado 23–15. "That was the start of something very, very good," said defensive back John Shelley. "That game was the bell cow for putting us over the hump." The Sooners later took eventual national champion Nebraska to the wire in Lincoln, then closed out the regular season by unloading on Oklahoma State 66–6. "By the end of the year, we were playing really well," Wylie said.

With an off-season to fine-tune the wishbone, the Sooners were a juggernaut waiting to explode. To begin the 1971 season, OU cruised past SMU, Pittsburgh, and USC to set up a showdown with third-ranked Texas. "We knew we were going to kick their butts," Crosswhite said. "We couldn't wait to play them."

Even though the Longhorns had created the wishbone offense, they didn't quite understand how to defend OU's breakneck

version of it. Texas lined up eight defenders between the tackles, which allowed the Sooners to have a numbers advantage on the corner on virtually every play.

Midway through OU's first drive, Mildren pitched left to Pruitt, who, with Roy Bell providing the lead block, raced 46 yards down the sideline. "We were running downhill from then on," Shelley said. Even without Wylie, who missed the game with a sprained ankle, the Sooners racked up 435 yards on the ground—the most a Darrell Royal defense at Texas had ever allowed—en route to a 48–27 pasting of the Horns. Pruitt alone rushed for 189 yards in the first half, and Mildren finished with 111 yards and two touchdowns. "It was as if the light company turned the electricity off on Benjamin Franklin," wrote Hurt, whose tune had changed from the year before. "Oklahoma turned Texas' own invention on Texas. And the wishbone offense never looked as lethal as it did on the artificial floor of the Cotton Bowl. The Sooner wishbone struck with a flourish and a fury."

OU jumped to No. 2 in the polls and would remain there until facing Nebraska in the "Game of the Century." The Sooners lost 35–31. But the second great Oklahoma dynasty was firmly in motion.

2000

OKLAHOMA	14	28	14	7	**63**
TEXAS	0	7	0	7	**14**

After almost a decade of relative mediocrity, the Sooners had returned. It was more than just a singular beatdown of Texas. It was a launching pad of the third Sooners dynasty. It charted

the path to the school's seventh championship. It helped ignite a fund-raising drive that built the upper deck of Gaylord Family–Memorial Stadium and erected an indoor practice facility. It was the impetus for what became the program of the decade. "The way they dominated the game in 2000 jump-started them," Texas coach Mack Brown would later say. "It gave them great confidence and national attention."

Going into the season, the Longhorns were overwhelming favorites to win the Big 12 South and a sleeper pick by national pundits to contend for the national title. Texas returned 16 starters, including quarterback Major Applewhite, the 1999 Big 12 Co-Offensive Player of the Year. Also at quarterback was "prodigy" sophomore Chris Simms, who would eventually unseat Applewhite for the starting job. Defensively, the Longhorns featured future Pro Bowl defensive tackles Casey Hampton and Shaun Rogers. Other future NFL starters littered the lineup, including cornerback Quentin Jammer, offensive tackle Leonard Davis, and wide receiver Roy Williams. OU entered the game 4–0, but the Sooners were untested and unproven under second-year coach Bob Stoops. It didn't take long, however, for the Longhorns to fail to live up to the hype, losing to Stanford 27–24 the second week of the season. The Horns still entered the Cotton Bowl with a 3–1 record and No. 11 ranking. OU, meanwhile, arrived with far less fanfare. The Sooners were undefeated, but their four wins were against UTEP, Arkansas State, Rice, and Kansas. The Longhorns had won three straight in the series and were expected to win again. "Nobody really gave us any respect," said Derrick Strait, a four-year starter at cornerback beginning in 2000. "Everybody gave Texas the hype. We had to earn it."

Oklahoma quarterback Josh Heupel rolls out, looking for a receiver in the second quarter during OU's 63–14 pummeling of Texas in 2000.

What no one outside the program could account for before the Texas game was the extraordinary chemistry of that OU team. Sure, there was talent. But it was also a ragtag conglomeration of passed-over Texans like Strait and Brandon Everage; holdovers from the John Blake era like J.T. Thatcher and Josh Norman; and junior-college nomads like Torrance Marshall and Josh Heupel. Because they had never had anything, the 2000 Sooners played as if they had nothing to lose. And, as a result, they didn't. "We were really emotional, really played with a chip on our shoulders," Strait said. "We had so much to prove."

That became quickly and painfully clear to everyone on the Texas side of the 50-yard line on a rainy afternoon. On OU's opening drive, Heupel fired a 29-yard touchdown to Andre Woolfolk over Rod Babers. Then an option pitch to Quentin Griffin made it 14–0. "They kept scoring, we kept punting," Simms said afterward.

"They ran basic lead to the open side, and Rocky Calmus goes in there, takes on the fullback, Torrance comes over and destroys the guard, and everyone else murders the running back for a two-yard loss on third-and-1," said Teddy Lehman, a freshman linebacker that season. "After that, you just knew this is what it's going to be like the whole game. And it was." Griffin's two-yard and four-yard touchdown plunges gave the Sooners a 28–0 lead. And turning the ball over. Calmus picked off Simms and returned it 41 yards for another touchdown, before the Sooners capped the scoring barrage with a Curtis Fagan eight-yard touchdown on an end-around. By halftime, OU led 42–7.

"There was no cheering in the locker room," Marshall said. "Nobody was satisfied. We wanted more."

Out of the locker room, the Sooners scored. And scored. And scored again. Had Stoops not called off the Schooner, OU might have dropped off what wide receiver Fagan was hoping for—"70 or 80." The Sooners piled up 534 yards—a record against Texas—with 245 on the ground and 289 through the air. Brown's postgame remarks said it all: "I want to apologize to all of the Texas fans, our players, and assistant coaches because I obviously did a poor job this week." Brown had plenty to apologize for. Texas was held to 158 yards total, including –7 yards rushing. OU scored on its first five drives, while the Sooners defense held Texas to one first down and forced punts on five of its first six possessions. "I thought we'd win the game. That shows you how far off I was," Brown said as he pushed his ball cap above his brow. "I felt very confident coming into the game, and we didn't do one thing right."

The Sooners did everything right. For Griffin, it was a performance for the ages; his six rushing touchdowns were a school record. Heupel proved just as brilliant, completing 17 of 27 passes for 275 yards.

After the game, Ryan Fisher and Reese Travis swiped the Ruf-Neks' oversized OU flag and planted it midfield. Al Baysinger rode the Sooner Schooner. And Stoops did something he hasn't done since. He cut his players loose for a couple of hours to hang out with their families at the Texas State Fair. "I had a burger there outside on the bench," Stoops said. "We

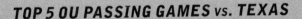

TOP 5 OU PASSING GAMES vs. TEXAS

1. **Sam Bradford** | 387 yards | 2008
   28-for-39, 5 TDs | 45–35 (Texas)

2. **Landry Jones** | 367 yards | 2011
   31-for-50, 3 TDs | 55–17 (OU)

3. **Josh Heupel** | 311 yards | 1999
   31-for-48, 2 TDs | 38–28 (Texas)

4. **Cale Gundy** | 276 yards | 1992
   17-for-38, 2TDs | 34–24 (Texas)

5. **Josh Heupel** | 275 yards | 2000
   17-for-27, TD | 63–14 (OU)

OKLAHOMA

sat on the bench for about two hours while the players tooled around. Sat there with our wives and coaching staff, and that was about it. We were off and back. Nobody really noticed us there."

The nation had taken notice after that. After a memorable run through "Red October," which also included victories over No. 2 Kansas State and No. 1 Nebraska, the Sooners knocked off Florida State to capture the school's seventh national championship. From there, OU became *the* dominant program in the Big 12. Since 2000, the Sooners have claimed seven conference titles—to just two for Texas—and captured nine of 13 games in the series going into 2012. "That game was a turning point for the whole program," OU safety Roy Williams said. "Changed everything."

1973

OKLAHOMA	7	14	14	17	52
TEXAS	3	3	0	7	13

With their flashy offense and even flashier coach, the Sooners flirted with greatness in 1971 and 1972 only to fall a game short of the national championship. Little did they know that in 1973 they were about to launch OU's second dynasty.

It's hard to believe now, but the Sooners entered the '73 season unsure of just how good they were. Gone were running backs Greg Pruitt, Joe Wylie, and Leon Crosswhite, who ushered in the wishbone era in Norman. Lightly recruited Steve Davis was a complete unknown at quarterback. And Barry Switzer was embarking on his first season as head coach.

Some pieces were already in place. The three Selmon brothers were about to start together for the first time on the defensive line. Joe Washington had shown flashes of brilliant running as a freshman the year before, and linebacker Rod Shoate had garnered All-America attention as a sophomore. But the voters were skeptical and in the preseason tabbed OU to finish *fourth* in the Big 8 Conference. The *Daily Oklahoman's* Bob Hurt wrote that if the Sooners didn't get past Baylor in the opener, they could easily head to conference play 1–3.

OU got past Baylor. But as the Sooners prepared for their second game at top-ranked USC, the NCAA slapped the Sooners with two years probation for recruiting violations, banning them from appearing on television in 1974 and 1975, and bowl games in 1973 and 1974. As OU traveled to Los Angeles, a

cloud hung over the program. Some predicted that the Sooners would get run out of the Coliseum.

Instead, the opposite happened. The Sooners completely outplayed the defending national champions, despite numerous self-inflicted mistakes. OU fumbled on its first three possessions, and later handed the Trojans their only score with a fourth turnover. OU more than doubled USC in total offense but missed two critical field goals and had to settle for the 7–7 tie. "They had some of the most premier players on that freaking team, and they weren't able to do nothing against us," said Washington, referring to Pat Haden, Anthony Davis, and Lynn Swann, USC's star-studded triplets. "We didn't realize how good we were until the USC game. We should have beaten them 35–0. That game just solidified what kind of team we had." The Sooners couldn't wait for another shot on the national stage. They would get it two weeks later in the Cotton Bowl.

Opposite its Red River rivals, Texas entered the season with immense hype. *Sports Illustrated* branded the Longhorns preseason No. 1, and Dave Campbell's *Texas Football* magazine projected the national championship would come down to the Horns and Notre Dame. But after hanging tough with USC on the road, the Sooners realized the best team in the country resided in Norman. It didn't take long for them to prove it.

After forcing Texas to punt, the Sooners quickly went to work. Washington sliced through a huge hole to the right 28 yards into UT territory on OU's first offensive snap. Five plays later, Switzer dialed up a halfback pass.

In August, Switzer had hired Jimmy Helms away from Texas to be on his staff. Helms brought with him a precious piece of inside information that the Longhorns overlooked in preparing for the game. After the Sooners went to the wishbone, Texas' secondary had been taught to key on OU's center. If the center showed run block, the defensive backs would fly up to the line of scrimmage. "Because of that edge, we knew they'd be susceptible to the play-action pass," Davis said.

With center Kyle Davis showing run, Davis flipped the ball to Washington, who had never thrown a pass in college. As the UT defenders pursued, Washington rose up and lobbed the ball 40 yards downfield to Tinker Owens, who was all alone. "It was the hardest catch I ever had to make," Owens said, "because there was nobody around." The trick play gave the Sooners an early 7–0 lead.

Texas hung around the first half with a pair of field goals. But like USC, the Longhorns failed to puncture OU's imposing front line defense. The Selmons—Lee Roy, Lucious, and Dewey—who together would finish with 17 tackles, plugged all holes up the middle, and Shoate ran down UT halfback Roosevelt Leaks whenever he tried to escape to the outside. "Once we stopped Roosevelt, it was pretty easygoing," said end Jimbo Elrod.

The OU offense, meanwhile, finally got rolling in the second quarter. Davis found Owens for a 63-yard scoring bomb. Then with just seconds to go before half, Davis lofted a 47-yard pass down the left sideline for speedy split end Billy Brooks, who snagged the ball between two Texas defenders before coasting into the end zone. The Sooners led 21–6 and never looked back. "That was pretty much a dagger in the heart there,"

Brooks said. "We knew against our defense they weren't going to be able to get back in the game."

Attempting just one pass, the Sooners marched down the field on the opening drive of the third quarter to make it 28–6. Then the OU defense began teeing off. In a matter of minutes, the Sooners knocked Leaks out of the game, forced two interceptions and two fumbles. When the dust finally settled, OU had a 52–13 victory—the worst defeat Darrell Royal ever suffered as coach of the Longhorns. "We came totally apart," Royal told reporters afterward. "Totally unglued." Royal's quarterback Marty Akins likened the loss to a "nightmare." "We kicked their ass," Washington said. "We could have played eight quarters, and they would have never scored more than 13 points. Our defense was that dominant." *Daily Oklahoman* sportswriter Frank Boggs, who had picked Texas to win, agreed. "When you stop to view the wreck you get the feeling the game wasn't really as close as the scoreboard indicates," he wrote. "It was more one-sided than a hanging."

The victory proved to be the launching pad for one of the greatest three-year runs in college football history. The Sooners mowed through the rest of their schedule to finish unbeaten for the first time in 17 years. "The game was just the galvanization of a program, a team," Davis said. "The biggest by-product of winning is confidence. Some call it swagger. The Texas game gave us that." Overcoming the probation, OU went on to win the next two national championships while extending its winning streak over the Horns to five games. "All of that started with the '73 win over Texas," Washington said. "That was the game that validated us."

TOP 5 OU RECEIVING GAMES vs. TEXAS

1. **Mark Clayton** | 190 yards | 2003
   8 catches, TD | 65–13 (OU)

2. **Corey Warren** | 187 yards | 1992
   9 catches, TD | 34–24 (Texas)

3. **Tinker Owens** | 163 yards | 1973
   4 catches, 2 TDs | 52–13 (OU)

4. **Aubrey McCall** | 130 yards | 1945
   7 catches, TD | 12–7 (Texas)

5. **Ryan Broyles** | 122 yards | 2011
   9 catches, TD | 55–17 (OU)

OKLAHOMA

1948

OKLAHOMA	0	7	7	6	**20**
TEXAS	0	0	0	14	**14**

In the 1940s morale in Oklahoma had been decimated. The Dust Bowl had devastated the land. The "grapes of wrath" had destroyed the pride. During a defining regents meeting at the University of Oklahoma, oilman Lloyd Noble suggested OU build up its football program to restore the spirit of the state. Noble argued that by hiring a football coach who could recruit World War II veterans—many had four years of athletic eligibility remaining—the Sooners could field a great football team overnight.

Before the 1946 season, the regents flew in Jim Tatum, who brought a prospective assistant coach with him to the interview. The two had coached together on one of the Navy's service teams. This prospective assistant, however, stole the show. And Noble was so impressed, he prodded the regents to offer Tatum the job—with the stipulation that he bring Charles "Bud" Wilkinson with him. After one season, Tatum left for Maryland, and Wilkinson was convinced to stay. Two years later, OU embarked on one of the longest winning streaks in college football history. Then, embarked on another.

The '48 season, however, did not get off to a promising start. OU flew to San Francisco for its opener against Santa Clara, which had won just four games the previous year and didn't have a staunch football tradition. The Sooners jumped to a 17–7 lead and appeared to be headed for an easy victory. But Santa Clara used two long completions in the second half to come storming back and stun the Sooners 20–17. "To this day, I still can't believe we lost that game," said Ed Lisak, an end on that team. "But it was the first time Bud had this particular bunch together. We were just feeling each other out." Especially two of OU's best players, quarterback Darrell Royal and center Buddy Burris. After the Santa Clara loss, Burris overheard Royal in the locker room say he didn't think he played as badly as the newspapers suggested. Burris turned to Royal, who had turned a receiver loose on the game-winning touchdown, and shouted, "Hell, Darrell, you played a lot worse!"

As the team prepared to go to the airport to fly back to Norman, KOMA sportscaster Curt Gowdy found Wilkinson sitting outside the visitors locker room with his head in his hands. "Tough loss, Coach," Gowdy said, trying to console

him. Snapping out of his funk, Wilkinson lifted his head up and said, "I'll tell you one thing: we may not lose another game in three years." He was right. And the victory that put the 31-game winning streak full throttle came two weeks later.

Despite the optimism for the '48 season, OU entered the Cotton Bowl huge underdogs. The Sooners had lost every game to Texas in the 1940s. The Longhorns were coming off a 10–1 season that included a 27–7 throttling of Alabama in the Sugar Bowl. But Texas had never faced an OU team with so much speed. The Sooners' moderate success the previous two years enabled Wilkinson to recruit playmakers OU had never possessed before. Slashing runner Jack Mitchell, who had actually played on UT's freshman team in '42 before the war, led the way. In the off-season, Wilkinson had moved Mitchell, who had led the Big 6 in rushing the season before, from quarterback to halfback and inserted Royal as the starting quarterback because he thought the Sooners needed to pass more. But after the Santa Clara debacle, Wilkinson realized how valuable Mitchell was as a running quarterback and prudently moved him back to his original position. "Jack was a great runner," said Claude Arnold, who took over for Mitchell at quarterback the following season. "He couldn't throw a lick hardly, but he didn't need to because our offense was primarily a running offense. He was an ideal quarterback for that system. A gifted runner and a great leader." Royal, fellow speedy halfbacks George Thomas and Buddy Jones, and rumbling fullback Leon Heath rounded out a backfield that was waiting to explode.

In pregame, Wilkinson reminded his players of what had transpired the year before. A couple of controversial calls by official Jack Sisco sparked UT's 34–14 rout of the Sooners in

a game that ended with OU fans hurling bottles onto the field. "He wasn't about to let us forget about that," halfback Tommy Gray said. "He reminded everyone how they had taken advantage of us and all that. He knew how to get people pumped up. We were all excited about the game, but especially the vets. They were hot about having lost the year before."

Before a record Cotton Bowl crowd of almost 70,000—the stadium had expanded in the off-season—the OU backfield finally exploded. Mitchell orchestrated the split-T rushing attack to near perfection, while linebacker Myrle Greathouse stifled the UT offense with tackle after tackle.

The Sooners took a 7–0 lead into halftime on Heath's two-yard touchdown plunge. Then, after a 66-yard drive, Thomas put OU up by two touchdowns on a short scoring run in the third quarter. Texas countered with a touchdown to cut the deficit, but the Sooners answered in just three plays. Mitchell gained six on a quarterback keeper, then Heath blasted through the right side 68 yards to the Texas 12. On the next snap, Thomas swept around the right end for a touchdown. Future Dallas Cowboys Hall of Fame coach Tom Landry scored for Texas, but it was too little, too late. Spearheaded by 338 rushing yards, including 214 by Heath and Thomas, the Sooners ended UT's dominance of the series with a 20–14 win. "Our biggest achievement to that point," tackle Dean Smith said.

After the win, Sooners fans from all around the Cotton Bowl poured onto the field and trampled down one set of goal posts. The next day, the *Daily Oklahoman* told of Sooners fans celebrating late into the night, even in locales where they weren't welcomed. Many congregated at the Mural Room in the Baker

Hotel, where the band kept playing "The Eyes of Texas" and, despite the many requests, refused to play "Oklahoma!" During the intermission, the band even had the audacity to unplug the microphone so OU fans couldn't use it. But Texas inhospitality couldn't tarnish this night. "For nine long years we waited for this," wrote Ralph Sewell of the *Daily Oklahoman* the next day. "Lean, hungry years they were, too, but tonight we quaff deep from the cup of victory."

After the game, Wilkinson and the players posed for a picture around the "Golden Hat." The snapshot has become a lasting depiction of the Sooners' unparalleled, decade-long run of dominance; in reality, the photo signified the beginning. Led by its dynamic backfield and stalwart tacklers Burris, Greathouse, and Buddy Jones on defense, OU blasted through the rest of the schedule. Only TCU and Oklahoma State on their home fields managed to play the Sooners to within a touchdown. OU won the Big 7 title outright to earn a chance to play North Carolina in the Sugar Bowl. The Tar Heels claimed All-America tailback Charlie "Choo Choo" Justice, but the Sooners defense as well as the flu slowed down Justice, and OU prevailed 14–6. The Santa Clara defeat seemed like a distant memory. "I never dreamed after that we would never lose another football game in my career," Royal said.

The Longhorns would only topple OU once over the next decade, which would include three Sooners national championships. "We were not as well organized from a football standpoint or from the standpoint of morale as we might have been the past few years," Wilkinson would later write. "This team laid the foundation, however, for the squads that we have had since that time."

1952

OKLAHOMA	28	0	0	21	**49**
TEXAS	0	7	0	13	**20**

As a coach, Bud Wilkinson was the total package. He was beloved by the Oklahoma administration, especially regent Lloyd Noble and president George Cross. He knew how to rub elbows with boosters, ultimately leading to the formation of the Touchdown Club. And he could recruit Texas better than those who coached in the state. But those who played for Wilkinson forever remember his masterful ability to whip his team into a frenzy with just a few words.

Before the 1952 Texas game, Wilkinson recognized his team had become too cocky. He became especially irritated when he saw underclassmen signing autographs in the team hotel. The night before, the players were joking and laughing as they waited to have a quick team meeting before going to the movies. Just then, Wilkinson barged in and said he was canceling the meeting. "The reason is because you're going to lose tomorrow," he said. "Not because you're not good. Because you think you're so much better than you are." Wilkinson went on to recite the parable "shirtsleeves to shirtsleeves in three generations," which tells of a family ending up where it started because the third generation believed everything was owed to them. "You think those kids wanted your autograph because of *you*?" Wilkinson asked. "They wanted it because you represent the University of Oklahoma." Wilkinson turned and tossed the chalk against the board, and as he walked out, said, "You don't deserve the money you got for your movie tickets, you

have not earned those clothes on your back, and you have not earned the right to sign an autograph for anyone."

The players sat in silence. Finally, quarterback Eddie Crowder and center Tom Catlin got up, put their 75¢ on the table and went to their rooms. The rest of the team followed suit.

"We were so goddamn embarrassed," recalled halfback Jack Ging, "but everything he said was so true." The first play of the game, Ging popped Texas halfback Jimmy Dan Pace so hard he fumbled. The Sooners recovered and quickly scored. Before the end of the first quarter, OU led 28–0 and went on to win 49–20. "We played like the first generation, not the third," Ging said. "The strings coach Wilkinson pulled were truths, not bullshit. We won that game the night before."

1956

OKLAHOMA	6	13	13	13	**45**
TEXAS	0	0	0	0	**0**

The 1952 game wasn't the only time Wilkinson pulled the right strings to get his team ready to play the Longhorns. In 1956 Wilkinson had his best team yet. OU came into Dallas riding a 32-game winning streak and had already hammered North Carolina and Kansas State by a combined score of 102–0. The Sooners had a hard time taking anyone seriously, including the Longhorns, whom they had defeated four straight times. Texas had fallen on hard times and would win just one game the entire season. Most oddsmakers favored OU by four touchdowns, and some more than that.

Fifteen minutes before kickoff the Sooners were waiting for their coach to come into the dressing room and deliver his pregame pep talk. Five minutes later, still no sign of Wilkinson. The players were getting antsy. Finally, he showed up. "Gentlemen," he said, "I think you know that you didn't practice well this week. But it is no disgrace to lose to a team such as Texas. Even so, when they beat you, just remember that you are still Oklahoma, and keep your heads held high." With that, Wilkinson turned and left the room, his players bubbling with rage.

"We came out on fire," said OU halfback Clendon Thomas. After Tommy McDonald returned the opening kickoff 54

A view of the field at the Cotton Bowl during the 1956 Red River Shootout, which Oklahoma won 45–0. Photo courtesy of Getty Images

yards, the Sooners zipped through the Texas defense into the end zone on seven plays, capped by Thomas' two-yard scoring plunge.

Even disinterested, the Sooners were just about unbeatable that season. They had four All-Americans in McDonald, linebacker Jerry Tubbs, and guards Ed Gray and Bill Krisher. Because they were so talented and so well-organized, they ran one of the most sophisticated offenses in college football history, including double reverses, Statue of Liberty plays, and swinging gates. "Bud would go into the dressing room before practice, draw some things on the board, and we'd go out to practice and run it perfectly on the first try," Krisher said. "The '56 team was just tremendous."

When the '56 Sooners were acutely interested, the only question was, how bad would the final score be? Spurred by Wilkinson's masterful use of pregame psychology, OU beat up the Longhorns in every facet of the game. The Sooners outgained Texas 369 yards to 74 on the ground, and forced seven turnovers. McDonald and Thomas each scored three touchdowns, as OU routed Texas 45–0—to that point the second-most lopsided score in the history of the rivalry. "A prairie fire called Oklahoma put the torch to Texas with such racehorse halfbacks as Clendon Thomas and Tommy McDonald as the main flame throwers," *Daily Oklahoman* sports editor John Cronley wrote afterward. "Oklahoma beat its ancient opponent seven ways from the ace."

Two weeks later OU did the same to Notre Dame, blasting the Irish 40–0. Up next was a road meeting at Colorado, a game the Sooners were hardly up for. It showed, too, as the Buffaloes

led 19–6 and threatened to derail the winning streak. But once again, Wilkinson had the magic touch. "Gentlemen," he said at halftime, "it's taken Oklahoma many years to build up its reputation, and you are letting that reputation down today. Take those jerseys off. You don't deserve to wear them." Then he exited the room, again leaving his players in silence. Minutes later, Wilkinson reappeared and said, "Gentlemen, there is only one person in the entire stadium who knows you are going to win this game. That's me." The Sooners made an honest man of their coach and roared back to win 27–19. Afterward, Wilkinson entered the locker room and said, "I think I've said enough today. I'll talk to you Monday." OU went on to capture its second straight national championship and extended the winning streak to 40.

1966

OKLAHOMA	6	3	3	6	**18**
TEXAS	3	0	0	6	**9**

In Oklahoma, they're known as the "four Bs." As in Bennie, Bud, Barry, and Bob. But take out Jim Mackenzie, and there wouldn't have been a Barry. And OU probably wouldn't be the program it is today.

In 1965 OU football was in turmoil. Gomer Jones, who had been at the ground floor at the building of the Sooners dynasty as Bud Wilkinson's most trusted assistant, gracefully resigned after only two seasons as head coach following a 3–7 season. The Sooners turned immediately to Texas coach Darrell Royal to resurrect the program, offering Royal a lucrative six-year contract that would pay him $32,000 annually. But Royal,

who grew up in Hollis, Oklahoma, then starred for Wilkinson in the 1940s, declined. "There'd be something lacking in a person, I think, to grow up in a state and go to that state university and not have some feelings and loyalties," Royal would say. "But, on the other hand, I think there'd be something lacking in a person who could come here...and be as deeply involved as I was, and not have some emotions here, too."

Unsuccessful in getting Royal to join them, the Sooners were desperate to find someone that could beat him. The Sooners had lost eight in a row to Texas, which remains tied for OU's longest losing streak in the series. OU pursued Georgia's Vince Dooley, but was turned down again. Then the Sooners finally found their man.

Jim Mackenzie was a 1952 graduate of the University of Kentucky, where he was an all-SEC tackle playing for Bear Bryant. Mackenzie was on the team that ended OU's 31-game winning streak in the 1951 Sugar Bowl. After a brief stint coaching high school and junior college, Mackenzie joined Frank Broyles' staff at Missouri in 1957. The following year, he went to Arkansas with Broyles, who turned the Razorbacks into a national power.

Under pressure to make a quick hire so that recruiting wouldn't suffer, OU president George Cross decided to make a run at Broyles' right-hand man—though getting him to Norman wasn't easy. Day after day, Cross tried to call Mackenzie, but could never get anyone on the phone. Cross then realized he had been calling an Arkansas student with the same name who had gone home for Christmas break. Through Broyles, Cross finally got in touch with Mackenzie the coach, who agreed to

interview for the job. Problem was, Mackenzie fell asleep on the way and didn't get off the plane in Dallas to make the connecting flight to Oklahoma City. When Mackenzie woke up, he was in Colorado Springs. Mackenzie called OU officials to apologize. Later, he jokingly said, "Well, I heard Royal didn't interview, and he was offered the job."

With him, Mackenzie brought a winning attitude and a star-studded coaching staff that would be the foundation of OU football for the next 25 years. Among those assistants were Chuck Fairbanks and Barry Switzer, future OU head coaches who were hell-bent on whipping the program back into shape. Immediately, Mackenzie and his staff attacked the recruiting trail like never before to restock the cupboard. In a matter of days, Mackenzie convinced future stars like fullback Steve Owens, ends Jim Files and Steve Zabel, and center Ken Mendenhall to attend OU. Mendenhall, an all-state star out of Enid, Oklahoma, had been leaning toward to Arkansas. But in one snowy night, Mackenzie changed his mind. "He called me after he had been named head coach," Mendenhall said. "I told him I had already made up my mind to go to Arkansas."

"Has your momma started supper yet?" Mackenzie replied. "Well, I'm going to get in my car now, and I'm driving up there." Mackenzie kept his word. He drove 100 miles through a sleet storm and took Mendenhall's family out to dinner at the Enid Holiday Inn. By the time dinner was over, Mendenhall was OU-bound.

"Frank Broyles wasn't going to drive through a sleet storm to get me," Mendenhall said.

Back in Norman, Mackenzie was instilling a similar intensity among the players. "The off-season program they implemented that spring was the most grueling we'd ever been through," said Bob Warmack, then OU's sophomore quarterback. "They didn't care if they ran people off—and they did. But those who made it through there were pretty much warriors."

Almost overnight, Mackenzie had transformed the mentality of the team. "He really did," said wideout Eddie Hinton, also a sophomore that year. "I wasn't used to losing, and I was very frustrated my freshman year. This wasn't the tradition of the school. I was thinking of maybe going elsewhere. But the first day, Coach Mackenzie said, 'We're all gonna start on the same line. And we're going to win.'" Mackenzie understood he had to make his players feel like winners, too. He put carpet and lounging chairs in the athletic dorms. He also changed the helmet color from white to crimson. "He put us in the mind-set we were going to be champions," Hinton said. Out of the gate, the Sooners rolled to convincing victories over Oregon and Iowa State, setting up the showdown with Royal's Long-horns. It had been seven years since OU scored more than a touchdown on Texas, but Mackenzie felt good about his club's chances. "The team is showing quickness, zip, and enthusi-asm," he told the *Daily Oklahoman* the week of the game.

Mackenzie also had something up his sleeve, besides his usual pack of cigarettes, to ensure his team was motivated. Early in the week, a voice identified only as "Texas Rose" went on a Norman radio station and ridiculed the Sooners. KNOR claimed Texas Rose had pirated its frequency. Turned out, with Mackenzie's approval, the ploy had been a hoax. Texas Rose was an OU Pi Phi named Marty Nelson.

On the opening drive, Texas looked unstoppable, despite not having star quarterback "Super" Bill Bradley, who injured his knee the week before against Indiana. The Horns methodically drove to the OU 3-yard line while also wilting six minutes off the clock. But on third down, Royal failed to send the play in on time, and Texas was flagged with a delay of game penalty. Andy White, Bradley's replacement, overthrew wideout Greg Lott in the corner of the end zone from the 8, and Texas had to settle for a field goal. The blunder by Royal proved to be a turning point. Granville Liggins and the Sooners defense dominated the rest of the afternoon, causing five turnovers. Warmack and the OU offense, meanwhile, got going. Late in the opening quarter, Warmack caught the Horns napping with a pass in the flat to a wide-open Ron Shotts, who rumbled 27 yards to the Texas 24 before being thumped out of bounds. Shotts then blasted through the right side for 22 yards to the Texas 2. Two plays later, Warmack faked to Shotts, then broke around the right on a naked bootleg.

"I just tried to put the ball on my hip to hide the ball from the people on the perimeter," Warmack recalled. "There was a defensive end kind of spying on me, and he saw that I had it. But as he came up to make the tackle, I cut up inside and got into the end zone before anyone else could get to me."

Place-kicker Mike Vachon pulled the extra point left. But that would be his last miss. Vachon connected on a 31-yard attempt to give OU a 9–3 lead just before half. Then to begin the third quarter, he nailed a 43-yarder into the wind for the longest field goal in OU history. The Sooners led 12–3 going into the fourth quarter, and 15–3 after Vachon added a 20-yard

field goal after Bob Stephenson's interception deep in Texas territory.

But for the first time since its opening drive, the Texas offense came alive. On third-and-10, White found Ragan Gennusa for an 18-yard strike to the Texas 42. White capped the drive with a two-yard scoring plunge. Even though the two-point try failed, Texas trailed just 15–9 with nine minutes go to despite being dominated for most of the game.

Warmack, however, answered with a 44-yard completion to the Texas 22, setting up one of the more bizarre back-and-forth sequences in college football history. All OU needed was another Vachon field goal to put the game out of reach. Instead, Shotts fumbled the ball to the Horns, and panic cascaded through the crimson side of the stadium. But on the next play, Texas running back Jim Helms fumbled the ball right back to OU. Except then, two plays later, Warmack bobbled the snap, and Texas recovered.

Two plays after that, White was picked off by OU linebacker Rickey Burgess, who returned the ball to the Texas 27 before he fumbled. Fortunately for the Sooners, the ball rolled out of bounds. The final tally was four turnovers on four fumbles and one interception in just over four minutes.

With 3:41 to play, Mackenzie wasn't about to squander his good fortune again. After three conservative run plays, he sent in Vachon for the game-clinching field-goal try. And from 41 yards out, the toe-poker from Amarillo, Texas, split the uprights again to seal the win. The streak was finally over.

Joyous players hoisted Mackenzie, Galen Hall, and Switzer on their shoulders and carried them away to the locker room.

"Now University of Oklahoma boosters can get excited about Jim Mackenzie's first football team," the *Daily Oklahoman*'s Volney Meece wrote. "Undefeated, untied, and largely untested after early-season brushes with Oregon and Iowa State, the Sooners stunned favored Texas 18–9 Saturday and erased several doubts about their prowess by doing it more convincingly than the score—lovely as it was to long-suffering OU faithful—hinted."

Back in Oklahoma City, thousands of flag-waving Sooners fans showed up on the tarmac at Will Rogers Airport to greet the team. Police tried to keep the fans behind the fences but were unsuccessful. There, Mackenzie was presented with a congratulatory letter from Governor Henry Bellmon. "Congratulations to each of you on a great win," the letter read. "You could not have won any sooner or better."

1996 (OT)

OKLAHOMA	0	13	0	11	6	30
TEXAS	10	7	0	7	3	27

The week of the Texas game, the Oklahoma Sooners were a downtrodden group. OU had lost all four of its games under first-year coach John Blake, and nobody gave the Sooners a chance in the Red River Rivalry. Anyone who watched OU's Friday walkthrough would have given the Sooners even less of a shot. The Sooners were so sloppy, offensive coordinator Dick Winder warned the next player who dared jump offside

would run every step inside Memorial Stadium. Moments later, freshman wideout Jarrail Jackson jumped. "We weren't focused or locked in, me especially," Jackson said. "I had to run every step in the stadium, in my cleats." The penance took Jackson almost an hour to complete. Without enough time to shower, a sweaty Jackson just barely made it onto the team bus as it pulled out for Dallas. Good thing for the Sooners they didn't leave Jackson home. They would need him.

In the 67 years that the Red River Rivalry had been played in Dallas in October, OU had never entered the game with four losses. Until the '96 season. The Sooners had been dreadful, losing to TCU, San Diego State, Tulsa, and Kansas by an average margin of 17 points. "The Red River Riot Might Be Rout," was the headline in the *Daily Oklahoman* the day of the game. Oddsmakers favored Texas by more than three touchdowns—the first time the Longhorns had been favorites since 1984. Blake, however, was not discouraged. "We might not have won a game right now, but this team has improved unbelievably," he said. "I'm truly excited about what is going on with this football team."

Realizing a win over Texas was the only thing that could salvage their season, the seniors called a team meeting in the dressing room before taking the field. "This is Texas, we're OU!" linebacker Broderick Simpson shouted. "We need to get our shit together for this game. This means everything. We're letting down the whole state. We're letting down the program."

Early on, it looked like the same Sooners. On its opening drive, Texas drove to the OU 34-yard line before committing an ineligible-receiver-downfield penalty. Blake elected to decline

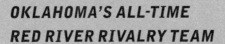

OKLAHOMA

OKLAHOMA'S ALL-TIME RED RIVER RIVALRY TEAM

OFFENSE

QB **Steve Davis** (1973–1975): Davis beat Texas three times while OU went on to win two national titles.

RB **Quentin Griffin** (1999–2002): The scatback scored a record six touchdowns in 2000, then rushed for 248 yards in 2002—both OU victories.

RB **Greg Pruitt** (1970–1972): Out of OU's wishbone, Pruitt lit up the Horns for 310 yards and four touchdowns in his career.

WR **Mark Clayton** (2001–2004): Clayton, who never lost to the Horns, hauled in a series-high 190 yards receiving in 2003.

WR **Ryan Broyles** (2008–2011): The FBS career receptions record holder hauled in three touchdowns in the series.

TE **Keith Jackson** (1984–1987): Jackson's 56-yard TD reception from Eric Mitchel put the Sooners up 31–0 at halftime in 1986.

OT **Jim Weatherall** (1948–1951): Weatherall played a key part in the series-changing victory in 1948 and kicked the game-winning extra point in 1950.

OT **Jammal Brown** (2001–2004): The Outland winner finished 3–0 as a starter against Texas.

OG **Bill Krisher** (1955–1957): Krisher won two national titles and went 3–0 against Texas.

OG **Anthony Phillips** (1985–1988): OU never lost to Texas when Phillips was on the line.

C **Tom Brahaney** (1970–1972): Brahney was an integral piece of the first OU wishbone offense that routed the Horns in 1971.

DEFENSE

DE **Jimbo Elrod** (1973–1975): Elrod's strip of Earl Campbell led to the game-winning field goal in 1974.

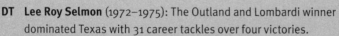

DT **Lee Roy Selmon** (1972–1975): The Outland and Lombardi winner dominated Texas with 31 career tackles over four victories.

DT **Derland Moore** (1970–1972): The former walk-on was a hero in 1972, blocking a Texas quick-kick for a touchdown, then returning a fumble for another score.

DE **Jimmy Wilkerson** (2000–2002): Wilkerson sacked Chris Simms three times as OU held Texas' high-powered offense to a mere field goal in 2001.

LB **Brian Bosworth** (1984–1986): The "Boz" led the OU obliteration of Texas' offense in both 1985 and 1986.

LB **Jerry Tubbs** (1954–1956): Tubbs intercepted three passes in OU's shutout victory in 1955.

LB **Rod Shoate** (1972–1974): Shoate overcame a shoulder injury to finish with 21 tackles and a key forced fumble in 1974.

DB **Tommy McDonald** (1954–1956): McDonald also scored five touchdowns in 1955, 1956 routs.

DB **Roy Williams** (1999–2001): Williams' "Superman" sack sealed OU's victory in 2001.

DB **Clendon Thomas** (1955–1957): The two-way standout also rushed for four touchdowns in the series.

DB **Rickey Dixon** (1984–1987): Dixon went 3–0–1 against Texas and intercepted two passes in the 1987 blowout.

SPECIAL TEAMS

K **Mike Vachon** (1966–1967): The straight-on kicker nailed a record four field goals in 1966.

P **Darrell Royal** (1946–1949): Also starred on offense and defense.

KR **Joe Washington** (1972–1975): "Little Joe" finished with 483 all-purpose yards in the series, not including a critical 76-yard quick-kick in 1975.

PR **Jarrail Jackson** (1996–1999): Jackson's 51-yard touchdown return sparked the Sooners to a dramatic come-from-behind victory in 1996.

the penalty, bringing up fourth down and a 47-yard field-goal try by Phil Dawson. Blake's hunch was off, as Dawson nailed the kick to give UT an early 3–0 lead.

The previous week, OU's special teams had surrendered *three* touchdowns against Kansas. Texas made it four in two weeks, blocking Brian Lewis' punt attempt for a touchdown later in the quarter. "On the outside looking in, we looked like a team that was done," said OU running back James Allen. "But we were still together as a team. The seniors kept saying, 'We cannot lose this game, whatever it takes, whatever has to happen.' It was our time to step up."

Allen's time, especially. The much-maligned former *Parade* All-American from Wynnewood, Oklahoma, who had been stopped at the goal line in '94, had lost his starting job to freshman De'Mond Parker. This, however, would be Allen's time. On OU's opening possession, the Sooners called a pass play designed for Allen that went for 21 yards. "I had that feeling. After that play, I told Coach Blake, 'You need to let me play today,'" Allen recalled. Blake had a feeling, too, and after the first quarter, decided to feature Allen at tailback the rest of the way.

With OU trailing 10–3 in the second quarter, Allen went left for 10 yards, then up the middle for eight. The Sooners offense was alive. "James was running like nothing I'd ever seen," said Jackson, who capped the drive with his first career reception, an eight-yard touchdown grab from quarterback Justin Fuente that tied the game with six minutes to go in the first half.

Allen and Jackson were just getting warmed up. But so was Ricky Williams. After a scoreless third quarter, Williams put

the Longhorns ahead 24–13 with a seven-yard scoring run through the middle of the OU defense.

Meanwhile, Texas governor George W. Bush exited the Cotton Bowl supremely confident the Horns would prevail. As he passed by Oklahoma governor Frank Keating on his way, Bush jested that he wanted ribs *and* chicken on the dinner bet the two had made on the game. Bush, and Keating, knew only a momentum-shifting play could save the Sooners from falling to 0–5. Bush wouldn't be in the stadium to see it.

Before taking the field for a punt return with just under seven minutes to go, Simpson declared to Blake that "this one is going back." Simpson then told Jackson "follow me." Jackson received the punt, rounded right behind a ferocious block from Simpson that took out two Longhorns, then outraced the coverage down the sideline for a 51-yard touchdown. "Nobody was catching me after I got behind the wall," Jackson said. The Sooners converted the two-point try and trailed by just a field goal. "Had he not returned that punt.... Just an awesome play, just what we needed," Allen said. "It was just a huge momentum swing. The turning point."

From there, Allen took over. After another Texas punt, the Sooners handed to Allen up the middle. He spun right to break loose from one tackler. Then spun left to shake another. Thirty-six yards later, the Horns finally brought him down. But not before he put OU in field-goal range. "James was tired," Fuente said, "but he just kept making plays." From 44 yards out, Jeremy Alexander, who had missed a potential game-winning field goal in a tie against Texas the year before, nailed this attempt from the right hash, sending the Red River

Rivalry to its first-ever overtime. And just like the fourth quarter, the overtime was all Allen.

After the Longhorns settled for a field goal, OU's overtime possession went like this: Allen, rush for 11 yards; Allen, rush for two yards; Allen, rush for two yards; Allen, swing pass for eight yards to the Texas 2. "When we were making the drive, [fullback] Dwayne Chandler kept saying, 'This is you. This is you,'" Allen said. On the fifth play, Allen took a pitch to the right, cut inside to his left, then dove across the goal line. Touchdown. Before Allen could look up to make sure he scored, he was under a dogpile. "I was crying for all my kids, but especially for James Allen," Blake said afterward. "He never quit."

Allen finished the game of his career with 159 yards rushing, 51 yards receiving, and the game-winning touchdown run, outperforming Williams, who would win the Heisman as a senior. "The thing that stuck out about James Allen was his determination," said UT defensive coordinator Gary Darnell. "What I saw was a guy running like he did at Wynnewood."

Months later, Bush made good on his bet, providing 1,500 pounds of Texas beef to hundreds of Oklahomans who gathered in Altus for the victory barbecue. "When I grew up, my mother told me not to bet," Bush said. "Nothing like eating a little crow on Oklahoma soil."

The Longhorns rebounded to win the inaugural Big 12 Championship Game. But contrary to Blake's prediction, OU did not improve or build off its stunning upset of the Horns. The Sooners won just two games the rest of the year. Two

seasons later, Blake would be fired after failing to generate a single winning season. Yet, when it comes to the '96 season, few remember the losses. Everyone remembers *the* win.

2003

OKLAHOMA	14	23	14	14	**65**
TEXAS	7	6	0	0	**13**

It's difficult to remember now, but the 2003 Red River Shootout actually had drama. Trailing only 14–7, Texas had driven inside the Oklahoma 10-yard line behind galloping freshman quarterback Vince Young, forcing Bob Stoops to pop an octave of aspirin. But as the Horns were about to tie the game, Brodney Pool popped Young, who coughed up the ball into the arms of cornerback Derrick Strait at the 2. Game, set, and match. Six touchdowns later, the Sooners exited the Cotton Bowl with an eye-popping 65–13 shellacking. "By 2003, we knew who we were, we knew who they were," Strait said. "We never expected to blow Texas out of the water like that. But we expected to win."

Strait was the epitome of OU's dominating run over the Longhorns early in the Stoops era. Overlooked by the Longhorns coming out of high school in Austin, Strait joined the Sooners, started as freshman, won a national championship, finished 4–0 against the Longhorns, and won the Jim Thorpe Award. Strait didn't have NFL-caliber physical ability. But in their four meetings, he obliterated Texas wideout Roy Williams, who would become the seventh overall pick in the 2004 NFL Draft. Williams never finished with more than 100 yards receiving against Strait, who capped his OU-Texas career in

Jason White winds up to deliver a touchdown pass during another Sooners pasting of the Longhorns in 2003, this time 65–13. Photo courtesy of Getty Images

'03 with 11 tackles, three pass breakups, and two fumble recoveries. In the opening minutes of the game, Strait also picked off a Chance Mock pass intended for Williams and returned it across the field 30 yards to set up the Sooners' first touchdown. "He's had a great career against everybody," coach Mack Brown would say, "especially us."

Strait, though, had plenty of help from one of the better defenses in OU history. Pool picked off a pass to go with

his forced fumble. Safety Donte Nicholson added a career-high 11 tackles. Three other players, including Butkus Award winner Teddy Lehman, forced fumbles. And defensive end Jonathan Jackson intercepted a pass tipped by Dusty Dvoracek and raced 21 yards for a touchdown. "We went out there and got turnover after turnover, big hit after big hit," Lehman said. "It was like a tidal wave." When the tidal wave subsided for halftime, OU led 37–13. "We played so well off each other," said fullback J.D. Runnels, who threw a block that sprung Renaldo Works into the open field for OU's first touchdown. "If you made a mistake, you were going to lose. If you made two, you were going to lose by 20." Texas committed six of those in turnovers and lost by 52—the largest margin of defeat for either side in the history of the Red River Rivalry. "When we got up two touchdowns, they were done," said receiver Mark Bradley. "They just wanted the game to end from that point on."

1986

OKLAHOMA	17	14	7	9	**47**
TEXAS	0	0	6	6	**12**

The state fair was going on outside the Cotton Bowl, but by the third quarter of the 1986 Red River Rivalry, the carnival was in full swing on the Sooners sideline. Quarterback Jamelle Holieway was talking to girls, munching on M&Ms, and giving television interviews. Linebacker Brian Bosworth, who played with the words "Texas" and "Fred Akers" painted on his shoes was signing autographs with his father. And the starting offensive line was mowing through hot dogs. "At halftime, we were already having fun on the sideline," Bosworth

would say. "That's kind of a bad thing to do, maybe, but we knew the game was out of hand."

The Longhorns knew it, too. But they couldn't do a thing about it. The Sooners had embarrassed Texas before and would again. But this was different. The Sooners knew *beforehand* they would rout the Horns. Bosworth suggested he wanted a "decisive" victory, predicting OU might win 63–0. Holieway proved to be a reliable trash-talking wingman. After the game, he called the OU-Texas rivalry a "myth." "We're going to win all of them in the next few years," he said.

Just two years before, Texas had been ranked No. 1 in the country going into its game with the Sooners. But by 1986 OU had surged by UT in compiling talent. Even Barry Switzer had to admit Texas talent wasn't what it used to be. "We scrimmaged against the ones in practice that week," Holieway said, "and when we got into that game, it was not anywhere near what we were facing in practice. We knew we could score at will against them."

With Holieway operating the wishbone like a wizard, OU scored on five of its six first-half possessions to take a convincing 31–0 lead into halftime. On the first two drives, Holieway pitched to '85 hero Patrick Collins for a pair of touchdowns out of the option. On the fourth drive, Holieway kept out of the option for a 21-yard score. Neither Collins nor Holieway was touched by a Longhorn on any of the three scores. "The offense got a couple of quick scores, and we knew we were in control of the game after that," Bosworth said.

Bosworth and his fellow defenders were just as dominating, holding the Longhorns to 29 rushing yards while sacking

Texas quarterback Bret Stafford five times. After Collins pranced 23 yards into the end zone for his third touchdown, the Sooners led 45–6 in the fourth quarter. By then, the party had already begun on the OU sideline. "I really blew it," Bosworth said afterward. "I predicted 63–0." Instead, OU had to settle for a final score of 47–12—its largest margin of victory in the series since 1973. Said Bosworth, "A lot of rednecks will be happy tonight because of this score."

2004

OKLAHOMA	0	3	3	6	12
TEXAS	0	0	0	0	0

As the team bus weaved through the Texas State Fair, J.D. Runnels noticed something very strange. The guy seated next to him didn't bother looking out the window. Didn't once take the headphones off. Most bizarre? This guy was a freshman about to make his Red River debut. "I was one of those guys when the stadium filled up I felt like I was going to throw up," Runnels said. "But this dude wasn't rattled one bit. He was completely focused. One of the few guys I saw who wasn't shaken by anything."

Before the 2004 season, Adrian Peterson arrived in Norman by way of East Texas as the most ballyhooed running back to sign with the Sooners since Marcus Dupree. After rushing for more than 5,000 yards and 50 touchdowns his final two years at Palestine High, Peterson was the consensus No. 1 overall recruit in the country. Texas wanted Peterson bad. But Peterson opted to go with the program the Longhorns couldn't beat. "I did dream about playing for Texas when I

was growing up, and I would probably be playing for the Long-horns if I knew they could be a consistent contender for the national championship every season," said Peterson, who had watched OU humiliate the Longhorns 65–13 the year before from the Texas sideline as Mack Brown's guest. "But the more that I started to look at things, the more my dream started to change."

Despite the hype surrounding his recruitment, the majority of the Sooners upperclassmen were skeptical Peterson could really be that good. Then came the first day of summer condi-tioning with strength coach Jerry Schmidt. The players quickly realized why Peterson had been given the nickname "All Day" growing up. "He blew us away," Runnels said. "He wasn't rattled at all by Schmitty, and that was rare." Peterson blew away the rest of Sooner Nation in the opener against Bowling Green. On his eighth carry, Peterson ran through four tackles and 35 yards for his first career touchdown. He finished with 100 yards on 16 carries, the most rushing yards by an OU true freshman in a season opener in 32 years. But the defining game of Peterson's career wouldn't come for another month.

The Sooners entered the Cotton Bowl with a four-game win-ning streak in the series, which included 49- and 52-point beatings. There were signs, however, Texas was turning the corner. The Longhorns had an elite running back of their own in Cedric Benson and an up-and-coming quarterback named Vince Young. Texas climbed to fifth in the polls and averaged better than 41 points a game. But as it would turn out, the Longhorns had lost this game when they had lost Peterson. "I knew that would be a big game for him just because he was a Texas kid," Runnels said. "A lot of great Texas running backs

Oklahoma running back Adrian Peterson blows by Texas' Brian Robison during the Sooners' 12–0 win in 2004. Peterson racked up 225 yards rushing on the day against the then–No. 5 Longhorns. Photo courtesy of Getty Images

that came to OU made the jump in that stadium. When you make your mark, you want to make it in that game." Peterson would more than make his mark. He would brand Texas

with a performance so devastating, voters around the country wanted to award him the Heisman Trophy then and there.

After Kejuan Jones got the start, Peterson stepped on the field on OU's second possession, which began at the Sooners 4-yard line. On a counter run, Peterson cut off Runnels' block, then dashed along the right sideline 44 yards before Michael Huff dragged him down. From there, the carnage only worsened. The Sooners had the reigning Heisman winner at quarterback in Jason White. But on this day, OU would ride the freshman. "Our team just got the feeling," Runnels said, "we're going to give him the ball and see if they can stop him." The Longhorns couldn't. Utilizing a blend of counters, toss sweeps, and misdirection pitchouts, Peterson feasted on Bevo for 225 yards on 32 carries. The Sooners controlled the clock, kept Benson and Young off the field, and steamrolled to a 12–0 victory, handing Texas its first shutout in 281 games. "Peterson's really good," Brown said afterward. "He's going to be a great player." Problem for Brown was, Peterson already was.

2

MOMENTS WE LOVE

SUPERMAN TAKES FLIGHT

In Oklahoma, it's just called the "Superman Play." And had OU safety Roy Williams listened to Mike Stoops, it never would have happened. But he didn't, and it did. And years later, the Superman Play remains the single most iconic OU-Texas moment north of the Red River. "I still remember it well," said Brent Venables, then OU's co–defensive coordinator. "A very special play." A special game, too.

Despite getting embarrassed 63–14 by OU the season before, the Longhorns entered 2001 with Bevo-sized expectations. After coasting through their first four games, the Horns were ranked fifth, setting up the first top-five OU-Texas matchup in 17 years. The Longhorns had their most talent in 17 years, too. Thanks to back-to-back-to-back top-five recruiting classes, Texas featured blue-chip quarterback Chris Simms, bell-cow running back Cedric Benson, prototypical wide receivers B.J. Johnson and another guy named Roy Williams (not to be confused with OU's Superman). Behind that foursome, the Longhorns put up 41, 44, 53, and 42 points in Texas' first four games. Against OU, they would put up three.

"We always have to hear about how they have the No. 1 recruiting class, but that really doesn't mean anything. You still have to put it out there on the football field," OU's Roy Williams said. "We heard them talking about how they were champing at the bit to play us. They were gung-ho about Chris Simms, who was supposed to lead the charge to them winning. They kind of downplayed us, as if we were nothing. But we weren't much for talking. We were going to let our talk be displayed out on the field."

Texas brought glitz. The Sooners brought grit. OU's offense was average. But its defense reminded fans of the Boz and Selmon defenses of years past. Linebacker Rocky Calmus won the Butkus Award. Teddy Lehman, who started next to Calmus, would win the Butkus two years later. Tackle Tommie Harris, free safety Brandon Everage, and cornerback Derrick Strait were eventual All-Americans. And then there was safety Williams, who could control a game at safety the way Brian Bosworth and Lee Roy Selmon could.

The OU defense lived up to such billing on this day. The Sooners offense struggled throughout, and would for much of the season. OU managed to gain only 206 yards the entire game though did get something going in the second quarter. Replacing injured starter Nate Hybl, backup quarterback Jason White sparked the Sooners in the second quarter. On fourth-and-2 from the Texas 30, Bob Stoops gambled and decided to go for it. On the option, White made a perfect pitch to Quentin Griffin, who raced 17 yards for the first down. White rushed for 11 on the next play, then pitched again to Griffin on the option for a two-yard touchdown run. That was all the scoring the Sooners offense did that day. But it proved to be enough.

Led by Williams, the Sooners completely dominated and demoralized the Texas offense. Outside a Dusty Mangum 27-yard field goal with 14 seconds left in the first half, the Longhorns got nothing. Texas rushed for just 27 yards. Simms was sacked five times and threw four interceptions, including three in the fourth quarter.

Cornerback Antonio Perkins made one of those picks in the OU end zone with just over eight minutes left to set up the dramatic finish. The Sooners drove the ball back into Texas territory but the drive stalled. Clinging to a 7–3 lead, the Stoops brothers elected to punt instead of calling for a 44-yard field goal. Tim Duncan had already misfired from 24 yards out that day. So out of field-goal formation, Duncan punted the ball, which appeared destined to roll into the end zone for a touchback. Instead, Nathan Vasher inexplicably dove to catch the ball at the Texas 3.

Utilizing the media timeout, the Stoops brothers discussed OU's next move. "Coach Mike said to Bob, 'I'm going to come after them—Slamdogs!'" said Venables, referring to a blitz that called for Williams to shoot the gap between the left guard and tackle. Mike Stoops had ordered the blitz earlier, but it had backfired. Williams had attempted to leap over a blocker and took a helmet to the groin, allowing Simms to scramble out of the pocket.

During the timeout, Mike Stoops pulled Williams aside. "We're calling Slamdogs, but you better not jump again," he ordered. "I was like, 'Okay, whatever,'" Williams said. "But I knew the B-gap was going to be wide open, and I knew it was going to be the running back, and I knew he wasn't going to

*OU safety Roy Williams leaps and knocks the ball out of Texas QB Chris Simms'
hand during the fourth quarter, creating an interception for teammate Teddy
Lehman, the key play in the Sooners' 14–3 victory over the Longhorns in 2001.*

hit me high, because I'd run him over. I knew he was going to try and cut me, so I was like, 'I'm going for it.'"

As Williams suspected, Texas running back Brett Robin tried to cut block. But he was too late—Superman was already in flight. Williams flew over Robin and slammed Simms' arm as he wound up, popping the ball into the air and into the arms of Lehman, who waltzed in for a touchdown to clinch a 14–3 victory. "It felt like I was in the air forever," Williams said. "I timed it perfectly. If [Simms] had gone back further, there wouldn't have been a Superman play." But he did. And there was.

LITTLE JOE MAKES BIG KICK

Among Joe Washington Sr.'s coaching precepts was the belief that versatile players made for great players. So growing up around their dad's high school practices, Joe Jr. and brother Ken worked on every fundamental imaginable. Running, catching, blocking, tackling, and—as the Longhorns would later find out—punting. Before developing into a Texas all-state halfback under his father at Port Arthur Lincoln High, "Little Joe" won a regional punt, pass, and kick contest—skills he would take with him to Oklahoma.

Two years after his halfback pass ignited a rout of the Horns, Washington's versatility would come in handy once again. The 1975 Red River bout featured another meeting of top-five teams. The Sooners were heavy favorites having defeated Texas four straight. But Darrell Royal had his best team in years, led by future Heisman Trophy–winning running back Earl Campbell and Marty Akins, UT's first All-America quarterback since Bobby Layne.

The Sooners took a 17–7 lead into the fourth quarter, thanks to Washington's nine-yard touchdown scamper. Texas, however, refused to go away. The Longhorns trimmed the deficit on Akins' pitch to halfback Jimmy Walker, who raced 25 yards for a touchdown. On the ensuing drive, OU fullback Jim Culbreath fumbled after taking a hit from Texas tackle Brad Shearer. The Horns recovered, and Russell Erxleben nailed a 43-yard field goal to tie the game with eight minutes to play.

The Sooners countered with a clutch touchdown drive to regain the lead, 24–17, then forced the Longhorns to punt. Except Erxleben's punt traveled 65 yards to the OU 8-yard line. After two plays, including a Washington fumble that OU guard Terry Webb recovered, the Sooners faced third-and-8 from the 10. With still almost three minutes left, the Horns were primed to get the ball back with excellent field position and a chance to tie.

Earlier that season, the Sooners had held an open competition at punter to replace John Carroll. Washington gave it a shot, but Tinker Owens won the job. Still, Barry Switzer recognized that his halfback wasn't half bad at it, and installed a quick-kick package with Washington, just in case. Washington, however, never believed the Sooners would actually call the play in a game, especially one of this magnitude.

Over the headsets, Switzer and offensive coordinator Galen Hall were going back and forth about what play they should run. Nothing seemed attractive. Then Hall said, "Coach, what do you think about the quick kick?" To Switzer, that sounded better than anything else they had discussed. "Fine with me,"

Switzer replied. "We've practiced it. We ought to be able to execute it. Let's do it."

After Steve Davis called it in the huddle, Washington retorted, "We're really going to do this?" Davis affirmed they were. "I was like, *Oh, man!*" Washington said.

Yet out of the wishbone, Washington took the direct snap, turned sideways, and with a sweeping motion smacked the ball. "I knew I hit that baby just right," Washington said. "I hit it as good as I ever did in practice. After the first hop, I knew it was going to roll a little bit."

Did it. The ball bounced near midfield, and rolled and rolled. The Longhorns didn't have anyone remotely deep enough to try a

TOP 5 OU RUSHING GAMES OF ALL-TIME

1. **Greg Pruitt** | 294 yards | 1971
   19 carries, 3 TDs | 75–28 at Kansas State (W)

2. **De'Mond Parker** | 291 yards | 1997
   31 carries, 3 TDs | 27–24 vs. Texas (L)

3. **Billy Sims** | 282 yards | 1979
   36 carries, TD | 24–22 at Missouri (W)

4. **Mike Gaddis** | 274 yards | 1989
   29 carries, 3 TDs | 37–15 vs. Okla. St. (W)

5. **Steve Owens** | 261 yards | 1969
   55 carries, 2 TDs | 28–27 at Okla. St. (W)

OKLAHOMA

return, either. "It caught us off guard," Royal would say. "It rolled until it quit rolling." Eventually the ball quit rolling, but only after it had gone 76 yards. "I couldn't see their faces because they all immediately turned to see how far that sucker would roll," Washington said. "But you could just tell they were in shock."

Instead of taking over around the OU 40, the Horns now had possession all the way back at their own 14. "They had 86 yards to go," Switzer said. "They're not going to do that against the Selmons." Texas lost seven yards on its next three plays, and OU got the ball back to run out the clock for its fifth consecutive victory in the series. "Once we got them in that field position with our defense, there was no way they were going to march down the field," said end Jimbo Elrod.

Washington's punt broke the modern OU-Texas record, and would propel the Sooners to their second straight national championship. Narrating the game the following week for the Longhorn Club, Royal finally came to the quick kick. After the ball stopped rolling, he said, "You can call in the dogs and piss on the fire now."

COLLINS TOUCHED, BUT NOT TACKLED

Oklahoma beat the hell out of Texas in 1984, but didn't win. One of the three worst calls in the history of the rivalry saved the Longhorns, allowing them another play to end the game with a tying field goal. "We still had a sour feeling in our stomach," said running back Patrick Collins, "because we got screwed out of the '84 game." In 1985 Collins and company would rectify that wrong, launching the Sooners to a four-game winning streak over the Horns.

In 1983 Collins was unequivocally the fastest high school athlete in Oklahoma, blazing to a state title in the 100-meter dash. Collins also was a game-breaking running back for Tulsa Booker T. Washington, and Barry Switzer couldn't wait to pair him in the wishbone with Missouri high school sprint champion Anthony Stafford. "It was so great to just watch them run," said quarterback Jamelle Holieway. "I would pitch them the ball and just watch. Poetry in motion." In 1985, however, Holieway had not taken over quarterbacking the Sooners yet. Instead, a homegrown, lifelong Sooners fan named Troy Aikman was operating the wishbone.

Once again, the second-ranked Sooners were beating up on Texas—with little to show for it. Fullback Lydell Carr lost the ball at the OU 7, and UT defensive end Kip Cooper scooped it out of the air, then lumbered for a touchdown to put the Longhorns up 7–0 in the first quarter. Cooper turned out to be UT's only offensive weapon.

Despite losing All-America nose guard Tony Casillas on the game's third play to a knee sprain, the Sooners completely obliterated the UT offense. Other than the Cooper fumble recovery, the Longhorns never made it past the OU 46-yard line and were held to four first downs and 70 total yards of offense—including −24 in the second. "It was the greatest defensive performance ever by an Oklahoma team since I've been here," Switzer said after the game. "And that's 20 years. And we did it without Tony Casillas, who is the best defensive player in this country at his position."

But there OU was in the fourth quarter, staring down the barrel of another tie. The wishbone had also been grounded, and

with his defense playing so well, Switzer was careful not to risk another turnover. "It was a defensive battle, they didn't give an inch, we didn't give an inch," Collins said. Texas' defensive game plan had been to keep Collins and Stafford from breaking off the big run. If the Sooners wanted to give the ball to the fullbacks, okay. "They wanted us to take the long road rather than give me or Stafford the corner," Collins said. "But Lydell Carr had really pounded them all game. They slowly began pinching in, pinching in, pinching in. Finally, we got them."

On the fifth play of a drive that began at the OU 40, Aikman faked the dive to Carr, then sprinted left. As cornerback Stephen Braggs broke down to take the quarterback, Aikman flipped the ball to Collins. "Troy to his credit got to the corner and sucked in the defense," Collins said. "I saw the strong safety [Gerald Senegal] coming for me, so I set my angle for the sideline and took off." Forty-five yards later, Collins was in the end zone. "The safety and the corner are reaching out for Collins," Switzer said. "The guy's hand just slides down his back, just touches him. But it wasn't touch football we were playing. It was tackle."

OU beat Texas 14–7, and later that season on virtually the same play, Collins scored the winning touchdown at Nebraska, sending the Sooners on to their sixth national championship. "We knew if you beat Texas, you have a chance at the national title," Collins said. "It was a great play and a great moment for us."

VESSELS COLLECTS FIVE

Keith Jackson, Jamelle Holieway, and Barry Switzer are credited with first creating "Sooner Magic" in the 1980s. But in

reality, the first glimpse of Sooner Magic goes back all the way to Billy Vessels, Claude Arnold, Bud Wilkinson, and the 1950 Red River Rivalry.

Oklahoma had won 23 consecutive games going in, including two straight over the Horns. But Texas was improved. The Longhorns were ranked fourth in the polls, one spot behind OU, and were only 6½-point underdogs. "Texas is the finest looking team I have ever seen," Wilkinson said. "We're lucky if Texas doesn't run us off the field. It will take a miracle for us to beat Texas this week." Wilkinson, of course, was never afraid to resort to hyperbole when describing an opponent. But the Sooners would end up needing that miracle, as well as the greatest run of Billy Vessels' Heisman career—a run for which he was appropriately compensated.

In the first half, Vessels and Texas fullback Byron Townsend traded touchdowns, leaving the game tied 7–7 late in the second quarter. The Longhorns, though, seemed poised to take the lead with the ball at the OU 1-inch mark in the closing seconds. The Horns tried halfback Lew Levine up the middle. But he was stuffed. Then they tried a quarterback sneak. But Ben Tompkins, too, was stuffed. Before UT could run another play, time expired.

As the players exited to the locker room, Texas guard Bud McFadin came across Wilkinson and told the OU coach, "You sure have some nice guys on your team." It's unclear if the consensus All-American was taunting Wilkinson or trying to be friendly. Either way, Wilkinson was livid at halftime. "If anybody ever tells me that again, none of you will be playing," he told his players. "Don't ever let that happen again."

The game remained tied until the fourth quarter when Bobby Dillon picked off OU halfback Dick Heatly's pass and dashed 45 yards down the sideline for a touchdown. UT, however, missed what would be a critical extra point.

On its next two drives, OU still failed to string together first downs. With under five minutes to go, Texas was about to punt the ball back from its own 16. As the Longhorns broke the huddle, OU defensive tackle Ed Rowland overheard one of the UT lineman ask another for the count. "On two," the other lineman answered. "Ed heard them say that," said former OU halfback Tommy Gray. "He knew the count." Making it even easier for Rowland, Texas only had 10 men on the field. As the Longhorns snapped the ball, Rowland was in front of Billy Porter, who bobbled the ball, then tried to run away. Porter didn't get far, as a host of Sooners took him down at the UT 11.

Two plays later, Wilkinson called 16-trap lateral. "It was a reverse play where I faked left and pitched back to Billy, who came back to the right," Arnold said. As he came back right, Vessels saw UT defensive tackle Bill Wilson standing in the hole. Instead of attempting to evade him, Vessels lowered his left shoulder and planted Wilson into the ground while keeping his own feet. A few steps later, Vessels spun between two more UT defenders and into the end zone. Jim Weatherall, who had missed a near-disastrous point-after try the week before against Texas A&M, nailed this extra point, and the Sooners prevailed 14–13. "Our boys have a world of heart," Wilkinson said afterward. "It took a fumbled punt to beat Texas, but it seems if you play hard enough, things like that will happen."

Publicly, Texas coach Blair Cherry praised OU's resolve. Privately, Cherry apparently wasn't so complimentary. "Those (bleepin') Sooners are the luckiest (bleepin') team I've ever seen play," Cherry reportedly said. "Buck up, Sooners," *Daily Oklahoman* sports editor John Cronley wrote in response to the alleged quote. "That's what they've been calling the Yankees for years."

Even though Vessels built a reputation as a home-run back, Wilkinson later called the 11-yard game-winner against Texas the best run of Vessels' career. "I'd never seen such a demonstration of determined running," Wilkinson said. As Vessels celebrated the touchdown, a fan reached out and offered him a $5 bill. According to teammates, Vessels accepted.

The media in Texas bemoaned the loss for weeks. *Austin American-Statesman* sports editor Fred Williams charged that the contest was the worst-officiated game in the Southwest in a decade, claiming the Horns had not only crossed the goal line at the end of the first half, but that Rowland had been offside on the blocked punt. In response, the *Dallas Morning News'* Bill Rives countered, "It does little good at this time to raise a 'we wuz robbed' cry. Even if the officials did miscall the plays concerned, Texas still—in the opinion of many persons who saw the game—should have won. The Longhorns failed to capitalize on their opportunities, while the Sooners cashed in on theirs. That's the story of the game."

The win over Texas propelled the Sooners to their first national championship. The Horns wound up winning the rest of their regular season games, too, but finished a spot behind OU in the polls. Despite guiding the Horns to a No. 2 final ranking,

Cherry was forced out of coaching by UT fans. He had committed an unforgivable crime. He had lost three straight to the Sooners.

BROOKS REVERSES THE OUTCOME

Billy Brooks rarely touched the ball playing split end in Barry Switzer's wishbone offense. But when he did, something spectacular usually followed.

Brooks grew up in Austin, Texas, but didn't have the grades in high school to play Division I football. Instead he went to Navarro Junior College for a year and finished with a 3.85 grade-point average. Then, like several others from Navarro, he transferred to Oklahoma. During the 1970s, the Sooners had so many impressive-looking athletes. But Brooks, who

TOP 5 OU RECEIVING GAMES OF ALL-TIME

1. **Ryan Broyles** | 217 yards | 2011
13 catches, 2 TDs | 47–17 at Kansas (W)

2. **Ryan Broyles** | 208 yards | 2010
9 catches, 3 TDs | 43–10 vs. Colorado (W)

3. **Manuel Johnson** | 206 yards | 2008
5 catches, 3 TDs | 35–10 vs. TCU (W)

4. **Juaquin Iglesias** | 191 yards | 2008
12 catches | 45–31 vs. Kansas (W)

5. **Mark Clayton** | 190 yards | 2003
8 catches, TD | 65–13 vs. Texas (W)

OKLAHOMA

was 6′3″ and 190 pounds, stood out. "When I first saw Billy, I was like, *Holy crap, no way am I beating this guy out,*" said Tinker Owens, a two-time All-American, who would rotate with Brooks at split end from 1973 to 1975. "He was built like a stallion. His hamstrings were like ham hocks hanging off." Brooks also lettered in track and could have started for the OU basketball team had he stuck with it. "Billy was electrifying," said quarterback Steve Davis. "It's unfortunate we didn't do a better job of putting the ball in hands more often." Brooks touched the ball only once in the '74 Red River Rivalry. But it was that touch that won the game.

Coming off three consecutive dominating wins over the Longhorns, the second-ranked Sooners entered the '74 game three-touchdown favorites. But after getting embarrassed by 39 points the season before, Texas was resolute to play the Sooners tough.

Headlined by Joe Washington, Barry Switzer had his fastest wishbone backfield yet, but the OU backs couldn't break off a big gain. And in the fourth quarter, Texas clung to a 13–7 lead. "Up to that point, we were trying everything," Washington said. "Nothing was working." Yet another OU drive had stalled. The Sooners faced third-and-7 on the Texas 40. Switzer initially sent Elvis Peacock in with the halfback-pass play, which OU had scored on against the Longhorns the year before. But assistants Larry Lacewell and Galen Hall recommended from the press box that they try a flanker reverse.

Davis took the snap and started left, with Washington as the decoy pitch back. The Longhorns, who had darted to Washington all afternoon, immediately pursued the same way. But

instead of pitching to Washington, Davis flipped the ball to Brooks going the other direction. The flanker reverse turned out to be the perfect call. The Longhorns had completely over-pursued. "They just caught us by surprise. We weren't expecting it," Texas defensive end Lionell Johnson confessed later. "When I saw what was happening, [Brooks] was already gone." Kyle Davis threw a key block to spring Brooks into the open field, leaving Sammie Mason as the last Longhorn with a chance to bring Brooks down. But Mason underestimated Brooks' speed and couldn't cut him off before he reached the end zone "My stride was so elongated, I could take three steps and gain 10 yards," Brooks said. "I had very deceptive speed. I wasn't Usain Bolt, but I was pretty damn fast. Once I got going, that was it." As Brooks crossed the goal line to tie the game, he spiked the ball and drew a 15-yard penalty on the kickoff. Nobody wearing crimson even noticed. "Such a huge play, when you think about it," Washington said.

John Carroll missed the extra point, but Jimbo Elrod jutted the ball from Earl Campbell on UT's next possession, and Brooks' roommate, Rod Shoate, fell on the fumble. OU's wishbone grinded its way down the field, setting up a Tony DiRienzo 37-yard field goal, as the Sooners escaped with a 16–13 victory. OU would go on to capture the first of back-to-back national titles.

A year later, at the end of OU's second title run, Brooks, who carried the ball only three times all season, romped 39 yards for a touchdown on the same play as the Sooners defeated Michigan in the Orange Bowl, 14–6. "When your opportunities are so rare, you're inspired to run as fast as you can and try to score,"

said Brooks, who finished his career with only 24 catches, but still made All-American and became a first-round draft pick of the Cincinnati Bengals. "I always felt like I would."

GOOD-BYE, MARCUS

"The Best Who Never Was" *was* against Texas in 1982.

Of all the players to sign with Oklahoma, none came with more hype than tailback Marcus Dupree. Not Jack Mildren. Not Billy Sims. Not even Adrian Peterson. In the town of Philadelphia, Mississippi, Dupree rushed for 5,283 yards and broke Herschel Walker's high school record with 87 career touchdowns. Dupree's college recruitment turned into such a madhouse that Willie Morris chronicled it in in the book, *The Courting of Marcus Dupree*, published a year after Dupree enrolled in Norman. Dupree narrowed his decision to OU, Texas, and Southern Mississippi. Longhorns coach Fred Akers desperately wanted Dupree and pulled out all the stops to get him. But so did Switzer, ordering assistant Lucious Selmon to camp out at the Downtown Motor Inn in Philadelphia for two months. Dupree ultimately signed with the Sooners after Sims—Dupree's boyhood hero—flew to Philadelphia to recruit him personally.

Switzer revamped his entire offense to feature Dupree's talents, scrapping the wishbone for the I formation. "I recruited a lot of big-time, blue-chip players, but not like Marcus," Switzer said. "The first day he joined our team, he was the best player on the field. Earl Campbell was the only other guy I ever saw who was like that—physically ready as a true freshman to be

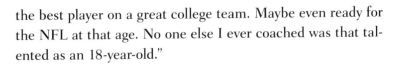

the best player on a great college team. Maybe even ready for
the NFL at that age. No one else I ever coached was that talented as an 18-year-old."

In the Cotton Bowl, Sooners fans finally saw why. OU was
mired in its only losing streak against the Horns in two
decades with Switzer as coach. Akers had bested his coun-
terpart three straight years, including a 34–14 thumping the
year before. But Akers was nervous about Dupree. And he had
reason to be.

Early in the first quarter, Dupree entered the game and carried
for seven yards. Then he took from quarterback Kelly Phelps,
faked a reverse handoff to Steve Sewell, slipped through a
tackle, cut left, and scooted down the right hash mark 63
yards for a touchdown. "Forty, 45, 50, open field! Forty-five,
40, good-bye, Marcus!" play-by-play man John Brooks bel-
lowed over the OU radio network. As he crossed the goal line,
Dupree raised his index finger, as if to signal his first touchdown. "I knew I could do it," Dupree later said. "I was doing it
against the first-team [OU] defense. I just had to get into the
flow of the game."

After Dupree's spectacular scurry, the Sooners never looked
back, rolling 28–22. Dupree capped his Red River debut with
96 yards rushing on only nine carries, as OU totaled 384 yards
on the ground. Dupree would go on to a freshman season for
the ages, rushing for 13 touchdowns while averaging a whop-
ping 7.8 yards per carry on the way to earning second-team
All-America honors. He finished the year by running for a
Fiesta Bowl–record 239 yards on just 17 touches. "Here he
was, a true freshman with that tremendous size, and people

OU halfback Marcus Dupree raises his finger in the air as he crosses the goal line, scoring his first touchdown in a 28–22 win over Texas in 1982.

just bounced off of him," said Merv Johnson, an OU assistant from 1979 to 1997. "Marcus' potential was limitless."

That potential, however, would be limited for good. Dupree's public rift with Switzer for criticizing him for being out of

shape in the Fiesta Bowl festered throughout the off-season. Before the '83 season, *Sports Illustrated* featured Dupree on its cover with the headline, "Clash of Wills at Oklahoma. Heisman Hopeful Marcus Dupree: Can He Coexist With His Coach?" In the end, he couldn't. In his second appearance against Texas, Dupree rushed for just 50 yards, the lowest output of his career as a starter, and suffered a concussion as Texas prevailed 28–16. After the game, Dupree disappeared to Mississippi, never to return to OU.

RICKY IGNITES GOLIATH

Never before, in 82 years, had one side of the Red River Rivalry been this big an underdog. In 1987 Texas, with two losses, was a 30-point dog to the Sooners. *Thirty.* OU, which had blasted UT by five touchdowns the year before, headed to Dallas ranked No. 1 in the country. The Longhorns limped into the Cotton Bowl having struggled to hold off lowly Rice the previous week. The *Dallas Times Herald* gave the Sooners the edge at every position, except special teams. "Texas is out of its league," *Times Herald* columnist Skip Bayless wrote the day of the game. "Texas is overmatched in both trenches, in experience, in greatness."

The Longhorns were overmatched, inexperienced, and definitely not great. But Randy McEachern, who came off the bench to quarterback the Horns to an upset victory a decade earlier, cautioned that OU-Texas was "made for Davids and Goliaths." And in the third quarter, the long-shot Longhorns were on the verge of proving McEachern correct. That was, until Ricky Dixon reminded David that he was in fact out of Goliath's league.

Scan the annals of OU history, and it's nearly impossible to find a player who supplied more big turnovers than Dixon. The Sooners' first Jim Thorpe Award winner and a consensus All-American in '87, Dixon came through with monumental plays against all three of OU's rivals. Against Oklahoma State, Dixon scooped up a tipped Mike Gundy pass and high-stepped down the sideline untouched for a touchdown to secure a 29–10 Bedlam victory. Two weeks later in the "Game of the Century II," Dixon picked off top-ranked Nebraska twice. The first set up OU's first score. The second sealed the 17–7 victory, catapulting the Sooners to the Orange Bowl.

Dixon dished out the dagger to Texas that season, as well. Despite being heavy favorites, OU struggled through the first half. The Sooners were so sloppy they even screwed up the coin flip. After the Longhorns won the toss and deferred, OU captain Greg Johnson had a brain freeze and said the Sooners would kick. Barry Switzer, who had ordered Johnson to take the ball, was incredulous.

Texas took advantage of the Sooners sleepwalk, and trailed just 13–6 at halftime. On the opening possession of the third quarter, the Horns drove all the way to the OU 14. "If they score there," Dixon said, "who knows what would have happened?" But UT would not score. On the next play, Texas quarterback Bret Stafford rolled right and flicked a pass in the flat to Jorrick Battle. Dixon read it the whole way. He broke in front of Battle for the interception, then streaked down the sideline with his patented high-step gait before being pushed out of bounds at the Texas 40. "I really thought we had a chance," UT coach David McWilliams said afterward. "We were moving the ball on them on that drive, and they couldn't

stop it. All of a sudden, they get the interception, and it turns it completely around."

Completely. The Sooners had been waiting for the right moment to pick on cornerback Tony Griffin, who played with a pulled Achilles tendon. They finally had it. Three plays after the pick, Jamelle Holieway tossed a 44-yard bomb to seldom-used wideout Carl Cabbiness, who burned Griffin for the touchdown. "You could just feel the game change there," Dixon said. "That killed all their momentum."

The oddsmakers would be proven wrong. They hadn't favored the Sooners by enough. Fueled by Dixon's pick, one of seven Sooners interceptions, OU exploded for three third-quarter touchdowns, and pasted the Horns 44–9—its second consecutive 35-point win in the series. "We were so good on both sides of the ball that year that once we made a big play and capitalized, it was like a train," Dixon said. "Once that train started moving…it was hard to stop."

STAFFORD SCAMPERS THE SIDELINE

From the moment he took over as offensive coordinator in 1967 to his final year as head coach in 1988, Barry Switzer enjoyed an embarrassment of halfback riches at Oklahoma. But the tandem Switzer enjoyed coaching most was not his most talented. "That was back when it was so great," Switzer said. "I didn't give a shit who carried the ball in that era, because I didn't have a prima donna at halfback. I didn't have a Marcus Dupree or a Billy Sims, someone I needed to get the ball in the hands of—Joe Washington—25, 26, 27 times. They didn't need to touch it that much."

They were Patrick Collins and Anthony Stafford. And they terrorized Texas through the mid-1980s. Collins hailed from Booker T. Washington High School in Tulsa. Stafford was from St. Louis. Neither was big or imposing. Stafford was just 5'7", 175 pounds. Collins wasn't much bigger at 5'10", 185. But both were former state track champs. And the two, along with quarterback Jamelle Holieway, could flat fly. "Coach called us the 'Smurfs' because we were all short and damn fast," Holieway said. "I was the slowest one in the backfield and I ran a sub 4.5. If I pitched either one of them the ball in the seam, they were gone."

But besides being diminutive speed demons, Collins and Stafford were the consummate team players. Neither ever clamored for the ball. They were ferocious blockers for one another. And they understood the wishbone attack as well as any back Switzer coached. "Stafford and Collins were so smart, like bullets, heat-seeking missiles in the blocking schemes," Switzer said. "I'd see them adjust off not taking this guy, knowing the fullback is getting him, peeling off to the safety—all of a sudden Jamelle is right behind him. It was so great to look and see what's fixing to happen and see us execute."

In 1985 OU and Texas were deadlocked 7–7 when Collins took an option pitch in the fourth quarter and swung down the left sideline for a game-winning 45-yard touchdown. "My dream was to one day be in a position to make a run like that," Stafford said. "And in '88 it happened for me."

That year, the Sooners were beginning a trend downward that would last for more than a decade. OU was still ranked No. 10 in the country heading into the Cotton Bowl, but the Sooners

LOVABLE EFFORTS *IN* LOSSES

1. De'Mond Parker, 1997

In 1997 Sooners running back De'Mond Parker was one penalty shy of pulling off arguably the greatest performance in Oklahoma-Texas history. Instead, Parker had to settle for greatest Sooners performance at the Cotton Bowl in a loss. Outperforming Texas' Ricky Williams, who also had a monster day, Parker rushed for 291 yards and three touchdowns on 31 carries in the 27–24 loss.

"I told De'Mond in the locker room, 'I've coached some good backs, but I don't know if I've ever coached a guy who fought as hard as you did,'" running backs coach Joe Dickinson said after the game. "It was the classiest effort. He did everything he could do to help us win the football game. I've had some guys go over 300 yards before, but not in gutsy, big games like that."

Neither OU nor Texas was any good that season. Both teams would go on to losing seasons. But each squad had one whale of a back. Williams gained 223 yards and two touchdowns on 40 carries, marking just the fourth time up to that point in major college history that two backs rushed for more than 200 yards in the same game. But Parker was the best player on the field that day. In the fourth quarter alone, he rushed for 124 yards and two cross-country touchdowns on just six carries, and came three yards away from breaking the single-game OU rushing record, set by Greg Pruitt at Kansas State in 1971. Parker easily could have broken the record. Instead, he had a 65-yard touchdown run and another 20-yard rush wiped out by penalties. After Parker's 66-yard touchdown with 2:42 left, Texas and Williams ran out the clock to preserve the win.

didn't have a Tony Casillas, Brian Bosworth, or Rickey Dixon defensively. "There just wasn't as much talent," said Stafford, who was in his senior year. But OU still had playmakers in its

2. Sam Bradford, 2008

Quarterback Sam Bradford was good in the 2008 Red River Shootout. Just not good enough to overcome OU's breakdowns on special teams and defense. Despite completing 28 of 39 passes for 387 yards and five touchdowns—the most yards and touchdowns of any quarterback in the history of the series—Texas knocked off the Sooners 45–35.

Bradford and the Sooners were salty offensively, marching down the field on their opening drive and scoring on a five-yard touchdown pass from Bradford to Manny Johnson. After Bradford connected with Broyles on an eight-yard score to open the second quarter, it seemed like OU was on the verge of blowing the game open. But on the next play, Texas turned the tide with Jordan Shipley's 96-yard kickoff return for a touchdown. And in the fourth quarter, Colt McCoy outgunned Bradford to seal the victory.

Bradford and the Sooners would get their revenge. OU edged out Texas in a three-way tie to claim the Big 12 South title, and Bradford edged out McCoy for the Heisman.

3. Steve Owens, 1967–1969

Oklahoma's Heisman running back never beat Texas. But he rushed for 100 yards three times in tough losses.

In 1967 the Sooners were edged 9–7 by Texas but went on to a 10–1 season, including an Orange Bowl victory over Tennessee. In 1968 OU again was tripped by the Horns, 26–20. In 1969 OU was defeated 27–17.

Still, Owens totaled 356 rushing yards and averaged five yards per carry in the three games.

backfield in quarterbacks Holieway and Charles Thompson, fullback Leon Perry, Stafford, and gifted Midwest City freshman Mike Gaddis, who had succeeded Collins at halfback.

The Sooners led 6–0 in the second quarter, when returner Glyn Milburn fumbled a punt deep in OU territory. One official ruled it Texas' ball. But another overruled the decision and declared Milburn's knee was down. OU had the ball, but with awful field position. "We were backed up," Stafford said. "We were just trying to get a couple of first downs." Instead they would get the longest run in OU-Texas history. Charles Thompson, who had replaced an injured Holieway at quarterback, allowed the Texas end to crash down on him before pitching the ball to Stafford. Gaddis cleared out the safety, and fullback Leon Perry locked up the nearest linebacker. "I fully expected Charles to keep the ball, but kept pitch relationship in case," Stafford said. "When I got the pitch against the boundary, I started up the field. Out of the corner of my eye, I saw Leon clear the way. His block tripped me up, but I caught my balance. It was open field after that."

Open field for an 86-yard touchdown. Stafford touched the ball only three other times the rest of the game. But his run triggered OU to its fourth straight Red River win, a 28–13 final score. After the game, Switzer handed out two game balls. One to Stafford. And one to the entire senior class, which included Stafford, for having never lost to Texas. "If you stand out in that game," Stafford said, "OU fans tend to remember you for a long time."

DeMARCO HURDLES into HISTORY

The losses in 2005 and 2006 were two of the worst for the Sooners. After Vince Young crushed Oklahoma 45–12, freshman Colt McCoy quarterbacked the Longhorns to another victory, 28–10. It had been almost four decades since Texas had

beaten OU by at least two touchdowns in consecutive seasons. Another humiliating defeat would hand the Longhorns complete control of the series for the first time since the 1960s.

Then DeMarco Murray dashed, hurdled, and sprinted. And UT's streak was on its way to an end. Several scores later, Murray would break Steve Owens' record for touchdowns by a Sooner. But nothing could top his 65-yard freshman scoring scamper, which returned the Golden Hat north. "It was a very emotional touchdown, very exciting—your first touchdown playing in that game," Murray said. "I'll remember it forever."

Two years earlier, Bob Stoops was on a recruiting trip to Bishop Gorman High School in Las Vegas to visit linebacker Ryan Reynolds. While in the Gorman basketball gym talking to football coach David White, Stoops witnessed Murray throw the ball over the backboard, wait for it to bounce off the wall underneath the backboard, then jam home the alley-oop to himself. "Tell that kid," Stoops immediately said to White, "he has a scholarship to Oklahoma."

Murray, billed as the heir-apparent to Adrian Peterson, was sidelined as a true freshman at OU because of turf toe. But, once on the field, it didn't take long for him to show off the athleticism that had Stoops offering him a scholarship on the spot. In the '07 opener against North Texas, he lined up as a wide receiver and scored his first career touchdown on a 44-yard end around. He finished off four more drives with short runs near the goal line to become the first Sooner to score five touchdowns in his debut. Murray was just getting warmed up.

Oklahoma running back DeMarco Murray crosses the goal line after breaking a game-changing 65-yard touchdown run against Texas in the third quarter of the Sooners' 28–21 victory in 2007.

Despite both being ranked in the preseason top 10, OU and Texas entered their game coming off losses. The Sooners were stunned by a late field goal in Colorado. Texas was shellacked by Kansas State. Neither team could afford another loss and seriously contend for the Big 12 South.

Late in the third quarter, the game was tied 14–14, and OU had just been bailed out by Curtis Lofton's strip of Jamaal Charles inside the Sooners 5-yard line. OU had been unable to get anything going on the ground, and starter Allen Patrick had to leave the game with an injury. The Sooners had been trying to run off-tackle all game to no avail. But offensive coordinator Kevin Wilson refused to give up on the run. So he called the stretch play off-tackle once again.

This time, Murray slipped past linebacker Rashad Bobino, who had been clogging the stretch play all game. Then tight end Joe Jon Finley cleared a path by clearing out UT's other linebacker Scott Derry. But the path included Finley lying on the ground. So at full speed, Murray leaped over Finley, then blazed past cornerback Marcus Griffin for the electrifying 65-yard touchdown. "You definitely feel momentum swings in the OU-Texas game from plays like that," Reynolds said. "You feel your whole sideline get up."

Boosted by the monumental momentum swing, the Sooners went on to beat Texas 28–21. After the game, Murray did a victory lap around the Cotton Bowl wearing the Golden Hat. He would do the same three years later. As a senior, Murray led OU to a win over Texas again, rushing for 115 yards and two touchdowns, including a 20-yard tightrope down the sideline equally as acrobatic as the one his freshman year.

WINCHESTER SEALS THE WIN

James Winchester's deep-snapping career got off to an ugly start. On his very first Sooners snap, Winchester sailed the ball over punter Mike Knall's head for a safety—Tennessee-

Chattanooga's only points in a 57–2 squeaker in the 2008 opener. "Kind of a bad way to start," Winchester said then. "But I'll be all right." Two years later, Winchester was more than all right, becoming the first deep snapper ever to get a special ovation walking into the Cotton Bowl tunnel.

Winchester grew up a Sooners fan in a Sooners family. His dad, Mike, was OU's starting punter in the mid-1980s. His older sister, Carolyn, played for the OU women's basketball team in the late 2000s. His younger sister, Rebecca, was a member of the OU rowing team. Despite being recruited by a couple of small colleges, the Washington, Oklahoma, native elected to walk on to the Sooners football team. "My family had a huge influence on how much I loved OU," Winchester said. "It was bred into me."

In 2010 OU was clawing its way into the national championship conversation after a 4–0 start. The Sooners were well on their way to 5–0 in Dallas after DeMarco Murray tight-roped the sideline for a touchdown that put the Sooners up 28–10 on Texas in the fourth quarter. OU was just one play away from putting the game away for good. That play would come. But not from the offense or defense.

With the maligned Garrett Gilbert at quarterback, the Longhorns suddenly came to life. Big pass plays to Cody Johnson and Malcolm Williams spurred a pair of Texas scoring drives, and the Longhorns trimmed OU's lead to 28–20. Yet the Sooners had the ball with only 1:35 remaining. But instead of forcing Texas to burn its timeouts, the Sooners inexplicably audibled to pass. Quarterback Landry Jones rolled right, smack into Texas linebacker Emmanuel Acho, and as Acho

went for the sack, Jones dropped the ball. Several Longhorns had a chance to make the recovery. But on the ground, Jones managed to tap the ball hard enough to push it out of bounds at the 6-yard line, giving the Sooners a chance to run another play, punt, and hope for a stop. "In the huddle, we were talking about how crucial it was going to be to flip the field," Winchester said.

The irony of Winchester's career—underscored by his first snap against Chattanooga—was that he had never deep-snapped before college. Winchester played wide receiver in high school, and was a quarterback before that. Those two experiences, however, would give him a unique skill set as a deep snapper. Before the '08 season, OU veteran deep snapper Derek Shaw suffered an ankle injury, leaving Bob Stoops

TOP 5 OU PASSING GAMES OF ALL-TIME

1. **Landry Jones** | 505 yards | 2011
   35-for-47, 5 TDs | 58–17 at Kansas State (W)

2t. **Landry Jones** | 468 yards | 2010
   37-for-62, 4 TDs | 47–41 at Oklahoma State (W)

   Sam Bradford | 468 yards | 2008
   36-for-53, 3 TDs | 45–31 vs. Kansas (W)

4. **Landry Jones** | 453 yards | 2010
   32-for-46, 4 TDs | 43–10 vs. Colorado (W)

5. **Landry Jones** | 448 | yards | 2011
   35-for-48, 3 TDs | 38–28 vs. Missouri (W)

OKLAHOMA

scouring his club for a replacement. "They said they needed somebody, and we really didn't have anybody," Winchester said. "So I thought, *Well, that's an opportunity for playing time.*" Because he had played quarterback, snapping came easy. Essentially, it was like passing the ball through his legs. With no other recourse, Stoops pegged Winchester the starter, and it didn't take long for Stoops to realize he had uncovered a special weapon. Most college deep snappers were linemen. Because Winchester had the speed of a wideout, he could cover ground faster than virtually any other deep snapper.

Aaron Williams discovered this painfully. Williams, who had ended Sam Bradford's college career the year before, was about to give Texas the ball at midfield, with plenty of time to score and send the game to overtime. Instead, he dropped the fair catch, and Winchester, who beat everyone else downfield, was there to pounce on the fumble. "I was hovering on top of him, and when I saw the ball hit the ground, I went to dive," said Winchester, who recovered two other fumbles in '10 and was actually tied for the national lead going into the final month of the season. "Joe Ibiloye hit Williams, so I could get on it. I knew instantly the game was over. I didn't know what else to do but to get up and take off running. It was unreal."

As the Sooners walked through the south tunnel, only three players received special ovations. Murray. Linebacker Travis Lewis. And the deep snapper. "It's something pretty special, growing up an OU fan, watching the amazing OU-Texas plays like Roy Williams diving over like Superman," Winchester said. "To be in on one of those plays…it was really special."

3

RED RIVER HEROES WE LOVE

ROD SHOATE

Some of the biggest hits Steve Davis took in his quarterbacking career came during a small-town Oklahoma high school game from a future Sooners teammate: Rod Shoate. "A ferocious hitter," said Davis, who played at Sallisaw, of Shoate, a standout at Spiro. "When he hit you, you knew you were hit."

At a college with a proud linebacker tradition, Shoate might have been the best. "Switzer called him the 'heat-seeking missile,'" Davis said. "He loved to deal out punishment." Shoate joined Buddy Burris as one of only two Sooners three-time All-Americans. "I've seen most of the great linebackers that have come through here," said OU halfback Joe Washington. "They were great players, but Rod Shoate, he had another gear."

Besides delivering countless bone-jarring tackles, Shoate had 4.4 speed and made hay roping down ball carriers, long before Lawrence Taylor made the speed linebacker en vogue. "He used that speed to get to the point of attack," said OU defensive end Jimbo Elrod. "Nobody could really deal with that in that day and age."

TOP 5 PASSING YARDS *IN A SEASON*

1. **Sam Bradford** | 4,720 | 2008
2. **Landry Jones** | 4,718 | 2010
3. **Landry Jones** | 4,463 | 2011
4. **Josh Heupel** | 3,850 | 1999
5. **Jason White** | 3,846 | 2003

Shoate played high school ball in Spiro, tucked a few miles away from the Arkansas border. In 1971 defensive assistant Larry Lacewell was putting the finishing touches on OU's recruiting class when he came across Shoate's tape. Lacewell thought he was evaluating Shoate as a fullback, and came away unimpressed. When Shoate's high school coach informed Lacewell he needed to watch Shoate's defensive tape, Lacewell was blown away. "He had great speed, played with great linebacker instincts," said Barry Switzer, who immediately offered Shoate a scholarship. "He was one of the great players we had at linebacker."

Even on a defense that featured the Selmon brothers, Shoate stood out. And, seemingly, he always saved his best stuff for the Longhorns. "In the midst of the guys coming from Texas to play for Oklahoma, Rod relished being from Oklahoma in that game," said Shoate's college roommate, split end Billy Brooks. "He really enjoyed making the big play, especially against them."

Shoate made plenty of big plays in the Cotton Bowl, but his performance in '74 was perhaps the most dominating defensive display in the history of the rivalry. He did it with only one good arm, too. Shoate injured his shoulder making an arm tackle in the first half, but sucked it up and played through it. "It was tough, but I didn't let it bother me," he said afterward. "After all, this was the Texas game."

Shoate finished with 21 tackles, broke up two passes, caused a turnover, and recovered Earl Campbell's fumble that led to the winning field goal, as the Sooners escaped 16–13. "We'd come back to the huddle, and you could just tell the shoulder was hanging," Elrod said. "But Rod was one tough hombre. He was all over the place. That was a phenomenal performance."

Shoate finished with 41 tackles in the series, and in three games with him in the lineup, the Longhorns crossed the end zone just twice. "We were all amazed watching him," Washington said. "Wasn't a better linebacker in the world."

JAMES ALLEN

The bus inched closer to Dallas. Past Purcell. Then Pauls Valley. Finally Wynnewood. The whole way down, James Allen had reflected on his football career, and what could have been. What should have been.

After perhaps the most prolific high school tenure in Oklahoma history, Allen arrived in Norman as OU's most celebrated tailback recruit since Marcus Dupree. After leading Wynnewood

to back-to-back state championships, Allen was named a *USA Today* and *Parade* first-team All-American in 1992.

But like Dupree, Allen couldn't live up to insatiable expectations. After getting stuffed at the goal line by Stonie Clark in the '94 loss to Texas, Allen became a fan and media scapegoat for the Sooners' on-field struggles. "To be *the* guy that got stopped, when the ball is in your hands against Texas—I never got over that," Allen said. "At that moment in my young career, I hadn't mastered the true mental toughness to be able to get up after failing in a moment that means so much to so many people. To get written off when you're still young, you love school—that was tough."

A punching bag for the media and fans following the "Stone Cold Stop," Allen contemplated a transfer. Instead, he stuck it out. But by his senior year in '96, he had lost his starting job to freshman De'Mond Parker. "It just wasn't what I had expected," he said. "I felt like the media always came down on me. I was very bitter about that."

Then the bus approached Wynnewood. "It reminded me of where it all started," Allen said. "I was just doing a lot of soul-searching. My senior year wasn't going how I planned. I knew this was the last time they would see me in this light. I didn't want to let them down. As we drove by, I got this energy, this spirit. I let everything go and had this peace with everything. Maybe my career at OU wasn't what I had wanted it to be. But I had a chance to make everyone there proud of me again one last time."

In the dressing room before the game, the soul-searching continued. "I remember telling myself, *James, if you're going to*

earn your respect back, if you're going to get your name back, this is the day," he said. "I didn't know how it was going to play out. But I was going out there with a vendetta."

Allen's career wasn't the only thing on the brink. The Sooners were 0–4 under first-year coach John Blake, making the Longhorns 22-point favorites. But this would be a day of redemption. Even though Parker finished with more than 100 yards rushing, Blake put the game on Allen's shoulders in the fourth quarter.

With OU trailing 24–21 late, Allen took a handoff up the middle. He spun away from one defender. Then spun the other way from another. Finally, the Longhorns dragged him down 36 yards downfield, well within field-goal range. The Sooners tied the game 24–24, ultimately sending it to overtime. "His performance was incredible, especially for a guy who had been through so many trials and tribulations," quarterback Justin Fuente said. "For him to come through and play like he did was really incredible."

Texas settled for a field goal on its overtime possession, handing OU a chance to go for the win. On three runs, Allen put the Sooners inside the 10. The next play, he took a swing pass from Fuente to the 2. Finally he had what he'd been hoping for since '94: a chance to beat Texas at the goal line. "I said to myself, *I'm not going to get stopped,*" Allen said. "*I don't care if I run into a Mack truck.*"

Allen took the sweep right. Just like '94, he cut back inside and dove toward the goal line. This time, he crossed it. "I knew I was in," Allen said. "It was surreal. When I say surreal, I mean it was like an out-of-body experience. It was total vindication."

Tight end Stephen Alexander nearly broke Allen's nose as he leaped on top of him, shouting, "James, you did it! You did it!" The rest of Allen's teammates followed. "James took us to victory. It was redemption for him," said receiver Jarrail Jackson, the other star of the game with two touchdowns. "Every day James had taken criticism. He had been through the fire. He deserved that moment."

"It was just sweet," Allen said. "For me and the fans. Think about all the crap all the true diehard Sooner fans had taken that week. Can you imagine how sweet it was for the OU fans who were there in that moment? It was sweet for the whole state, the university." Above all, for Allen.

DERLAND MOORE

Oklahoma was going through a regular Friday Texas walk-through before traveling to Dallas. But as coach Chuck Fairbanks was about to dismiss the players so they could load the bus, defensive coordinator Larry Lacewell spoke up. "Just in case Texas comes out and tries to quick-kick, let's do something to be prepared for it," Lacewell told the team, curiously. As the Sooners went through their quick-kick defense, Lacewell passed by defensive tackle Derland Moore and suggested that Moore slide a step to the middle, between the guard and tackle. "Who knows? Maybe you'll mess up their blocking," Lacewell said. Such a subtle suggestion would forge Moore's career path going forward.

The Poplar Bluff High football field has since been named after Moore, but he was hardly a star there. Growing up at the foothills of the Ozarks in southeast Missouri, Moore spent far more

OU HEISMAN TROPHY WINNERS

Player	Position	Year
Billy Vessels	Running back	1952
Steve Owens	Fullback	1969
Billy Sims	Running back	1978
Jason White	Quarterback	2003
Sam Bradford	Quarterback	2008

OKLAHOMA

time working his dad's 2,000-acre wheat farm than playing football. Moore's top high school sport was actually shot-put. He set his high school's record in the event and qualified for the regional junior Olympic meet, which in 1969 was held in Norman. "This might be hard to believe, but I had never heard of the University of Oklahoma or the Sooners," Moore said. "I thought there were Indians still running around there. That shows how worldly I was growing up in the Missouri Ozarks."

Only Memphis State had even offered Moore a partial track scholarship. But, after a few minutes watching Moore throw, OU track coach J.D. Martin gave him a full ride on the spot. Paul Moore wanted his son to stay in Missouri, but when Moore told him he was also going to walk on to the OU football team, a compromise was reached. But it didn't take long for Moore to try and break it. "I quit after the first day," Moore said. "But when I told my dad what I had done, he basically told me, if I didn't get my ass back there, I had better be able

to whup his ass." Besides being a farmer, Paul Moore was a state trooper and a lieutenant colonel in the Missouri National Guard. "I knew he meant business," said Moore, who figured he'd have better luck sparring with OU's offensive line. Instead of taking on his father, Moore returned to practice intent on pummeling everyone else. "I was pissed off," Moore said. "I went out there with an attitude. I must have gotten into 13 fights that day." Moore had one memorable skirmish with fiery tight end Steve Zabel. "Here's Steve Zabel, first-round draft pick, big, tough sonofabitch, and this freshman goes toe-to-toe with him," Barry Switzer said. "Man, he was tough."

That's essentially how Moore fell in love with football. It's also how the Sooners fell in love with him. Immediately after practice, Lacewell called Moore up to the coaches' office. Moore thought he was getting the boot. Instead, Lacewell talked him into going on football scholarship.

By 1972 Moore had become one of the anchors on a defensive front that included Lucious, Dewey, and Lee Roy

OKLAHOMA

TOP 5 TACKLES *IN A* SEASON

1. **Jackie Shipp** | 189 | 1981

2. **Daryl Hunt** | 177 | 1976

3. **Steve Aycock** | 175 | 1970

4. **George Cumby** | 160 | 1979

5. **Daryl Hunt** | 159 | 1977

Selmon. "Derland gets lost in the conversation because of the Selmons," said halfback Joe Washington. "But he was a really good player." The Sooners had destroyed the Longhorns 48–27 the year before and were unbeaten and ranked second heading into the Cotton Bowl. Texas was better in '72, but Darrell Royal knew he was outmanned. So the week of the game, Royal installed the quick-kick to give the Longhorns a chance of controlling the field position. If Texas encountered any hopeless third-and-long situations, quarterback Alan Lowry would punt the ball away, eliminating the possibility of a turnover or punt return. Royal didn't know it at the time, but the Sooners would be waiting for it.

The week of the game, oil man and longtime Lacewell acquaintance Lonnie "Wolfman" Williams found his way into Texas' practices. Rumor has it that he posed as a construction worker, a perfect disguise with Texas' stadium under renovation at the time. Surreptitiously, Williams took in everything the Longhorns did, including the covert quick-kick, and reported back to Lacewell. "Darrell four years later in '76 accuses us of spying," Switzer said. "When the press and people were asking me—it's semantics here—'Did you spy on them? Did your staff spy on Texas?' 'No.' I was an assistant coach in charge of the offense when we spied on them. Chuck [Fairbanks] was the head coach. So did my staff spy on them? 'Hell no, they didn't.' But I didn't volunteer that, in '72 under Chuck, we did."

As Royal had anticipated, the game turned into a defensive struggle. Despite forcing five turnovers, the Sooners clung to a 3–0 lead in the third quarter. With Texas facing third-and-16 at its own 25, Royal called in the quick-kick. To his

horror, the OU defenders began hollering "Quick-kick!" before Texas even broke the huddle. The safeties ran back for a return, and Moore, recalling Lacewell's instruction, cheated inside. On the snap, he barreled past All-America tackle Jerry Sisemore and the guard untouched to block the punt. Defensive end Gary Baccus cleared out Lowry, allowing Lucious Selmon to pounce on the ball for a touchdown. Royal was dumbfounded. "I know a lot of folks who paid $7 will question the quick-kick," he said afterward. "I didn't think it would be expected."

Moore, who finished with 10 tackles and also forced Lowry into an interception, put the finishing touches on his career performance in the fourth quarter. Off a stunt, Baccus knocked Lowry's option pitch attempt to the ground, shooting the ball all way to the Texas end zone. Moore gave chase and fell on it for OU's second defensive touchdown, putting the Sooners ahead by the final score of 27–0. All told, the OU defense blocked a punt, intercepted four passes, recovered four Texas fumbles, and scored two touchdowns while handing the Longhorns their first shutout in 101 games. "Our defense played its finest game of any defensive unit I've coached at the University of Oklahoma," Fairbanks wrote the following week in his newsletter. "Our defense not only held Texas scoreless, but it was directly responsible for all three of our touchdowns, two of them outright."

After the game, Moore began to suspect the impetus for his good fortune. "I kinda figured something was up when, after the game, Coach Lacewell said, 'Now don't tell the press we worked on blocking that quick-kick,'" Moore said. "I kinda felt bad, but it was just one of those things that happened."

TOP 5 INTERCEPTIONS *IN A* CAREER

1. **Darrell Royal** | 18 | 1946–1949

2. **Rickey Dixon** | 17 | 1984–1987

3. **Sonny Brown** | 16 | 1983–1986

4*t.* **Darrol Ray** | 15 | 1976–1979

   Zac Henderson | 15 | 1974–1977

OKLAHOMA

The defeat proved to be devastating for the Longhorns. Texas won every other game, and could have contended for a national title had it not been for the loss to OU. Instead, USC captured the national title, and the Longhorns finished third in the polls, a spot behind the Sooners.

Moore went on to national acclaim after his Texas performance. He was named the Associated Press' national lineman of the week, and would later become an All-American and second-round draft pick of the Saints. "The weird thing is, that [punt block] really propelled me into the national limelight," he said. "Probably responsible for me becoming an All-American and a real high draft choice."

JOE WASHINGTON

His shoes were silver. And his moves were sweet. But contrary to popular legend, Joe Washington didn't pick Oklahoma over Texas because Barry Switzer had agreed to let Washington wear silver shoes, while Darrell Royal had refused. Shoe color

ultimately had its impact on Washington's decision. Just not silver ones.

Washington actually never wore silver shoes playing for his father at Port Arthur (Texas) Lincoln High School. The first time he wore them was in a Texas high school all-star game, long after he had already signed with the Sooners.

The Longhorns had wanted Washington badly, and Washington had grown up a diehard Texas fan. He watched the *Darrell Royal Show* religiously, and when "The Eyes of Texas" boomed from the TV, Washington would rise and place his hand over his heart. So how did this Longhorns lover end up playing for Texas' archnemesis?

For one, the Washington family grew close to Wendell Mosley, Greg Pruitt's high school coach, who had taken a coaching at job at OU and had been recruiting Washington for the Sooners. Mosley talked the family into visiting Norman—though only after they had seen a dozen other colleges. The weather also happened to be nice during the visit, and Washington was pleased to learn he would be able to wear his high school No. 24 at OU, since the player who had previously worn it was graduating. But what really caught Washington's eye? "I liked the fact that they wore white shoes," he said. "If you wore white shoes, you were real flashy."

Washington flaunted plenty of flash on his way to becoming a two-time All-America halfback for the Sooners. He finished his career with more than 4,000 rushing yards and scored 43 touchdowns, which included dozens of dazzling cuts, spins, and hurdles. "He was so unpredictable as a runner, you

Oklahoma running back Joe Washington (24) leaps high for a first down against Texas in the fourth quarter of the Sooners' 16–13 win in 1974.

couldn't tackle him," said Steve Davis, Washington's quarterback. "He had this ability to start and stop, the ability to do pirouettes, and do some of the most bizarre moves you could ever imagine."

Not only was he one of the best running backs in Sooners history, Washington was the program's best all-around athlete since triple-threat Tommy McDonald. "I played racquetball against Joe all the time," said teammate Billy Brooks, who was a first-round NFL Draft choice. "And even though I was much faster than him, I never beat him. Not one time. No matter where I hit it, he always found a way to get to the ball."

Texas never beat Washington, either. And "Little Joe" always found a way to make the big play against his former favorite team. "Whenever you needed Little Joe," said safety Zac Henderson, "he would show up."

In the 1973 meeting, Washington flicked a halfback pass to Tinker Owens moments before half, igniting OU's eventual 52–13 rout of the Longhorns. Two years later, he broke Texas hearts again, this time with a 76-yard quick-kick in the final three minutes that effectively iced the victory. "He was a complete football player," defensive end Jimbo Elrod said. "It didn't matter what it was, he could do anything that a coach wanted him to do."

Washington finished his career 4–0 against the Longhorns, and 43–2–1 overall, which included back-to-back national championships. A month after sealing the '75 Texas victory with the quick-kick, Washington saved OU's season at Missouri with a 71-yard cutback touchdown run on fourth-and-1, followed by a leaping dive over the goal line for the two-point conversion to give the Sooners a 28–27, come-from-behind victory. "He had this nervous hum about him, and the louder he hummed, you knew the more excited he was to play," Davis said. "Joe was a thrill to play with."

JERRY TUBBS

Legend has it that Jerry Tubbs never lost a football game until the pros. A good tale. But untrue. Tubbs actually lost three times at Breckinridge High School. But at Oklahoma, Tubbs never did lose. With Tubbs manning linebacker from 1954 to 1956, the Sooners surrendered an average of 2.3 points a game to the Longhorns, and 5.9 points to everyone else. "What a middle linebacker he was," said the other star of that era, halfback Tommy McDonald. "Speed. Quickness. And he had attitude."

In '55 Tubbs unleashed one of the greatest individual defensive performances in the history of the Red River Rivalry. On the third play of the game, Tubbs picked off UT quarterback Joe Clements' first pass. Two plays later, McDonald was in the end zone on a 28-yard scamper. With OU leading 13–0 in the third quarter, Tubbs intercepted Clements again. "He was like a defensive back when he dropped back the way he'd swivel his hips," said halfback Carl Dodd. "He acted like a halfback when he made those interceptions, dodging those tackles and running downfield."

After halfback Bob Burris fumbled, Tubbs came up with his third and final interception of the game to demoralize Clements and the UT offense. The Horns never crossed the OU 29-yard line and finished with just 61 yards rushing. "Jerry came into his own that game," Burris said. "It was the best game he had had up to that point, and he would have a lot of great ones after that."

Tubbs' three interceptions remain an OU-Texas game record. On top of that, he led OU with a game-high 27 tackles, as

OU NATIONAL AWARD WINNERS

Lombardi (Best Lineman or Linebacker)

Lee Roy Selmon	1975	Tommie Harris	2003
Tony Casillas	1985		

Butkus (Best Linebacker)

Brian Bosworth	1985	Rocky Calmus	2001
Brian Bosworth	1986	Teddy Lehman	2003

Outland (Best Lineman)

Jim Weatherall	1951	Greg Roberts	1978
J.D. Roberts	1953	Jammal Brown	2004
Lee Roy Selmon	1975		

Davey O'Brien (Best Quarterback)

Jason White	2003	Sam Bradford	2008
Jason White	2004		

the Sooners rolled 20–0. In the locker room with reporters, Wilkinson put his arm around Tubbs and said, "Here's the boy who did it for us today. Every time I looked, there he was with the ball in his arms.... That was the single greatest game ever played by an Oklahoma defender. I have never seen anything like it, nor will I ever see anything like it again."

Tubbs earned back-to-back consensus All-America honors his final two seasons and was the leading vote-getter in both the UPI and AP All-America ballots. He also became the first Sooner to win the prestigious Walter Camp Award as college football's outstanding player of the year. Despite playing center and middle linebacker, Tubbs finished fourth in the

Walter Camp (Player of the Year)

Jerry Tubbs	1956	Billy Sims	1978
Steve Owens	1969	Josh Heupel	2000

Nagurski (Best Defensive Player)

Roy Williams	2001	Derrick Strait	2003

Thorpe (Best Defensive Back)

Rickey Dixon	1987	Derrick Strait	2003
Roy Williams	2001		

Maxwell (Player of the Year)

Tommy McDonald	1956	Jason White	2004

Bednarik (Top Defensive Player)

Teddy Lehman	2003

OKLAHOMA

1956 Heisman voting, behind McDonald, Tennessee's Johnny Majors, and winner Paul Hornung of Notre Dame. Tubbs and McDonald, who split the regional vote, led OU to a 40–0 rout of Hornung's Irish that same year.

After getting drafted in the first round by the Chicago Cardinals, Tubbs was selected to play in the prestigious Chicago Charities College All-Star Game against the defending-champion New York Giants. As center, Tubbs was asked to handle snaps for the field goals, extra points, and punts for the college all-stars, whose punter was Hornung. During their practice, Tubbs' first snap rolled back to Hornung. Then the second. And the third. "This guy is an All-American," Hor-

nung later admitted to thinking, "and he can't even get a snap to me in the air." After another bad snap, Tubbs turned around to Hornung to apologize. "Sorry about this…but we never punted at Oklahoma."

TOM CARROLL

In 1950 Coach Bud Wilkinson was elated about the potential of a pair of halfback prospects. One would go on to become Oklahoma's first Heisman Trophy winner. The other would start one game in his entire career. But one game is all Tom Carroll needed to become an OU-Texas hero.

Carroll grew up in Okemah, Oklahoma, home to folk music legend Woody Guthrie. After a spectacular high school career, Carroll enrolled at OU in 1949 with another small-town Oklahoma prep star, Billy Vessels of Cleveland. In spring practice the next year, Carroll was so impressive some considered him to be the better runner of the two. Especially after he famously chased down OU star halfback George Thomas from behind on a 74-yard run during the annual varsity-alumni game. "It was a really close call between Vessels and Carroll," said Richard Ellis, a teammate of both. "Tom was very, very good."

Carroll, however, never stepped on the field that season. On top of playing football, Carroll was also in the Oklahoma National Guard and was called to service as a communications sergeant in an all-vehicle army reconnaissance outfit after war erupted in Korea. Vessels, meanwhile, became a sensation on OU's first national championship team. "Tom was a good talent and a really good guy," said Claude Arnold, OU's quarterback in 1950. "The timing just wasn't right for him."

Carroll, however, wouldn't let a war stop him from playing football. As the war wound down in '52, Carroll returned to Norman and rejoined the team, only to find he was hardly the same player. "I didn't even make the traveling squad," said Carroll, who had gained 40 pounds while serving in the military. "I was way out of shape."

Carroll, who got the ball just twice the entire '52 season and failed to letter while Vessels captured the Heisman, was determined to get back on the field. During the winter, he went out for track and ran the hurdles. During the summer, after his daily 45-minute drive back from working the oil fields in St. Louis, Oklahoma, during the summer, Carroll stopped by the football field and ran up and down the stadium steps for hours before finally going home. "Football became work, hard work," Carroll said. "I was tired all the time."

Thanks to that hard work, the weight poured off, and the speed came back. But in the fall, Carroll was still an afterthought in the minds of the OU coaching staff. Jack Ging and Larry Grigg were named the starting halfbacks. Carroll remained on the bench. "I wasn't sure I'd ever get to play again," Carroll said.

His time was coming. Two weeks before Texas, the coaches had the players run stadium steps for conditioning. Carroll was right next to All-America end Max Boydston, who had built a reputation as the top-conditioned athlete on the team. Carroll, though, had been running stadium steps every day for eight months straight. This was Carroll's turf. He zoomed past Boydston and every other Sooner up and down those steps. "I turned a lot of heads that day," Carroll said. "They didn't

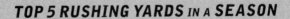

OKLAHOMA

TOP 5 RUSHING YARDS IN A SEASON

1. Adrian Peterson | 1,925 | 2004

2. Billy Sims | 1,896 | 1978

3. Quentin Griffin | 1,884 | 2002

4. Greg Pruitt | 1,760 | 1971

5. Billy Sims | 1,670 | 1979

know I had been running steps every day." That weekend, Ging suffered a separated shoulder against Pittsburgh, leaving the Sooners with a vacancy at halfback. After a war and thousands of steps, Carroll was finally in the lineup.

Early, after an exchange of punts, Texas began to put a drive together with three consecutive six-yard runs. On the fourth play, though, Carroll sliced through the Texas backfield and intercepted a lateral intended for halfback Billy Quinn to give the Sooners the ball at the Texas 25-yard line. "We had worked on that all week long," Carroll said. "Coach told us, 'If you're careful, you can intercept one of those pitchbacks.'" Five plays later, Grigg plunged over the goal line for a one-yard touchdown. The Sooners led 6–0.

In the fourth quarter, Carroll struck again, this time on offense. With OU leading 12–0, Carroll took a pitchout, raced around right end, broke Langford Sneed's arm tackle and dashed into the open field. Near the Texas 20, Don Brown cleared out the last remaining defender between Carroll and the end zone,

and Carroll showed his speed had come back as he outraced the field for the game-clinching, 48-yard touchdown. "Carroll's sudden bolt to stardom is one of those uphill success stories which is heart-warming to all concerned," *Daily Oklahoman* sports editor John Cronley wrote. "No one has worked harder or been more patient or persevering than Tom Carroll."

Carroll finished the day with a team-high 69 yards on 10 carries and was the talk of the Sooner State. But the fairy tale wouldn't last. The following week, Carroll blew out his knee, effectively ending his football career just as it was getting started. As it turned out, Carroll's one start was the first in OU's famed 47-game winning streak. "That one game against Texas," Carroll said, "that was my whole career." What a game. What a career.

MIKE VACHON

Before he was the Red River goat, Mike Vachon was the Red River hero. Such is life as a place-kicker.

Vachon grew up in Amarillo, Texas, and came to Norman with dreams of being the next Sooners quarterback. "Mike was just too slow. He just didn't quite make the cut as a quarterback," said Bob Warmack, who ended up winning the starting job. "But he wanted to play badly enough, so he tried kicking." Vachon wasn't the most conventional place-kicker. He wore the No. 92 and toe-poked the ball. "He wasn't too bad," Warmack. "He turned out to be the best that we had."

But in 1966, going into his first Texas game, OU coach Jim Mackenzie was a nervous wreck about his kicking game. "If

anyone had told me we'd outkick Texas," Mackenzie would later say, "I would have said they'd be smoking marijuana."

Vachon didn't evoke further confidence during pregame warmups. In fact, he missed everything. Then after OU scored its first and only touchdown in the first quarter, Vachon shanked the extra point wide left. "I wasn't hitting well in pregame practice," Vachon would say. "But when I missed [the extra point], I made up my mind I had a job to kick and not worry about it."

What followed was one of the greatest field-goal-kicking displays in OU history. With 17 seconds left in the first half, he toed the ball through from the 21 to give the Sooners a 9–3 halftime lead.

In the second half, Vachon was unconscious. On its opening possession of the third quarter, OU drove to Texas 24 before the drive stalled. Instead of going for it on fourth-and-long, Mackenzie—probably against his better judgment—opted to give Vachon a shot. Into the wind, Vachon smashed the ball through the uprights from 43 yards out. To that point, it was the longest kick ever made in the rivalry, and the longest kick in OU history. More importantly, it put the Sooners up by two scores, 12–3. "Mike was pretty erratic at times," Warmack said. "But that day he was on."

After a Bob Stephenson interception, Vachon added another field goal, this time from 20 yards away. It looked like that might be enough. But OU would need one more Vachon toe-poke to put the game away. Texas quarterback Andy White, who started for the injured Bill Bradley, finally got going

early in the fourth quarter. He capped a nine-play, 67-yard drive with a two-yard scoring run. White's two-point pass attempt failed, but UT was within striking distance, trailing only 15–9.

The Sooners, however, answered. Warmack found Ben Hart for a 44-yard completion all the way to the UT 22, before one of the craziest course of events in the history of the rivalry ensued. OU fumbled to Texas. Texas fumbled to OU. Warmack fumbled back to the Horns. Then White tossed an interception to OU linebacker Rickey Burgess, who amazingly fumbled on the return. But the Sooners caught a break, as the ball rolled out of bounds. All of this occurred in four minutes. After three cautious running plays, Mackenzie sent Vachon in to ice the game. Vachon did just that with a 41-yard conversion, his fourth field goal of the game, which would also be a school record. The Sooners won 18–9 in what would be the Sooners' only victory of the rivalry between 1958 and 1970. "This is the happiest day of my life," Vachon declared afterward.

TOP 5 RECEIVING YARDS IN A SEASON

1. **Ryan Broyles** | 1,622 | 2010

2. **Mark Clayton** | 1,425 | 2003

3. **Ryan Broyles** | 1,157 | 2011

4. **Juaquin Iglesias** | 1,150 | 2008

5. **Ryan Broyles** | 1,120 | 2009

OKLAHOMA

Vachon's magical season would continue. Seven weeks later, he nailed the game-winning field goal with 48 seconds remaining to upset fourth-ranked Nebraska on national television. Vachon also shattered the season school record with nine field goals. "Mike had ice in his veins that season," Warmack said. "Nothing fazed him. He was clutch."

But the fairy tale would not last. The following season, Vachon fell into a funk early on and couldn't shake out of it. He missed all five of his field-goal tries leading up to the Texas game, then in the Cotton Bowl misfired on both tries, including a 28-yard attempt late in the fourth quarter that would have given the Sooners the win. Instead, OU lost 9–7.

The following season, Bruce Derr took Vachon's place as field-goal kicker. "It was really unfortunate he went from the hero in '66 to the goat in '67," end Steve Zabel said of Vachon, who passed away in 2005 after a bout with colon cancer. "He was devastated. I'm sure he took that to his grave."

Vachon might have been the goat in '67. But he also gave OU its biggest win of the 1960s.

TOMMY McDONALD

The only man to get the best of Tommy McDonald turned out to be Oklahoma strength coach Port Robinson. Before Christmas break in 1955, McDonald had violated team rules, for which the standard punishment was running stadium steps. McDonald was never one for rules. And instead of checking in with Robinson to do his steps, McDonald slipped out of town after his last class and caught the first bus home to Albuquer-

Oklahoma quarterback Tommy McDonald led the Sooners to back-to-back national championships in 1955 and 1956. He would later become the first OU player to be inducted into the Pro Football Hall of Fame.

que. Robinson, an Army captain who had stormed Omaha beach during World War II, was livid. But McDonald was also the team's star player. So Robinson went to Bud Wilkinson to see what should be done. "Port, do what you feel is right," Wilkinson replied. That's all he needed to hear. Robinson telephoned McDonald's mother in New Mexico, and McDonald was on a bus back to Norman. The Longhorns wouldn't have such luck corralling McDonald.

After growing up in a small town in New Mexico, McDonald's family moved to Albuquerque his junior season. There, McDonald caught Wilkinson's eye running Highland High School's single-wing offense. McDonald was a five-tool player. He could run, pass, catch, block, and tackle. McDonald's best asset was his blinding speed. The second was his vice-grip hands, which he built up working with his dad, an electrician. "It made my wrists very, very strong when I would catch the ball," McDonald would say. "With me working with a screwdriver and doing a lot of outlets in houses, it made my fingers really strong."

McDonald was obsessed with scoring. He kept a little book with all his individual statistics, which drove his teammates into orbit. During scoring droughts, McDonald repeatedly pestered quarterback Jimmy Harris for the ball. But Wilkinson also appreciated McDonald's bluster. On the first kickoff return of his first scrimmage as a Sooner, McDonald went nowhere and was gang tackled. After practice, Wilkinson found McDonald tearing up to the side. Why did he get upset? He thought he had let Wilkinson down by not scoring a touchdown that play.

In 1955, with a team full of veterans, Wilkinson was inspired by McDonald's hustle to install one of college football's first

hurry-up offenses. After every play, McDonald sprinted to the huddle, then after every huddle, to the line. Other players followed suit. Soon, the whole team was sprinting between plays, leaving opponents gassed and confused. "Tommy McDonald is a funny kid," Wilkinson would say of the hurry-up. "He thinks he should score every play. When he doesn't, he gets mad and wants another crack at it. It's something God gave him. We didn't do it. The other boys picked up on it, and now the coaches are encouraging it."

Texas had no answer for such firepower moving so fast. McDonald scored early with a brilliant 28-yard touchdown scamper to the right. Then, later in the first half, he picked a pass and retuned it all the way to the Texas 7. The next play, McDonald took it into the end zone himself, as OU coasted 20–0. "Oklahoma's golden boy set a furious scoring pace for the second straight week Saturday as the Sooners, throwing the book at Texas from start to finish, again grabbed off the brass ring in this state fair feature," *Daily Oklahoman* sports editor John Cronley wrote.

The following year, McDonald astounded the Cotton Bowl crowd even more. He returned the opening kickoff 54 yards up the middle to spark the second-most lopsided score in the history of the rivalry to that point. McDonald ended up with two rushing touchdowns, and hauled in one of the most acrobatic touchdown grabs in Sooners history, thanks to those strapping wrists. He stabbed the rear third of the ball to make the catch before racing 53 yards for a touchdown seconds before halftime. OU rolled on, 45–0. "He caught it over his shoulder, his arm stretched out," said Sooners halfback Jakie Sandefer. "I remember thinking, *How lucky can a guy be?*" None of it was

luck. All told, McDonald outgained Texas' entire team with 140 yards rushing, 61 receiving, and 27 passing, and would lead the Sooners in all three categories on the season.

McDonald won the Maxwell Award and placed third in the Heisman voting. He might have won it had he and teammate Jerry Tubbs, who was fourth in the balloting, not split the vote. McDonald earned more first-place Heisman votes than anyone, including winner Paul Hornung.

After leading OU to back-to-back national championships, McDonald was drafted by the Philadelphia Eagles and in 1998 became the first Sooner to be inducted into the Pro Football Hall of Fame.

QUENTIN GRIFFIN

Quentin Griffin never much cared for statistics. Despite the fact that he racked up quite a few against Texas.

In the final game of his college career, Bob Stoops offered Griffin the opportunity to break the single-season OU rushing record. Griffin said thanks, but no thanks. In the Sooners' 34–14 Rose Bowl rout of Washington State, Griffin had rushed for 144 yards, leaving him 12 shy of Billy Sims' 1978 record of 1,896. With a minute left, Stoops tried to persuade Griffin to go back in and break the record. Griffin declined. "He wanted to see the other guys play," Stoops said. "Special young man."

Nowhere was Griffin more special than in the Cotton Bowl. Griffin, who was part of Stoops' first recruiting class in 1999,

TOP 5 TDS SCORED IN A CAREER

1. **DeMarco Murray** | 65 | 2007–2010

2. **Steve Owens** | 57 | 1967–1969

3. **Billy Sims** | 53 | 1976–1979

4. **Quentin Griffin** | 51 | 1999–2002

5. **Ryan Broyles** | 48 | 2008–2011

OKLAHOMA

wasn't even considered a top 100 prospect in Texas, in part because of his 5'7" frame. But the Aldine native was a perfect fit for the spread scheme Mike Leach was implementing in Norman. Griffin was a superb receiver out of the backfield, and would end up setting a school record with 169 career receptions. He was also incredibly durable for his size and would finish his career without having missed a single practice. But Griffin's No. 1 advantage was his shiftiness to make the first couple of defenders whiff.

As a sophomore, Griffin earned a starting job and went on to one of the finest careers by an OU back ever, despite playing on a pass-first offense. As good as he was against other opponents, Griffin will forever be remembered for the two record-setting performances he unleashed on the Longhorns.

In 2000 he rushed for a school-record six touchdowns in a 63–14 rout of the Horns. The win catapulted the Sooners all the way to the school's seventh national championship. Two

years later against Texas, he was even more spectacular. In the weeks leading up to the 2002 OU-Texas game, Griffin's touches had gradually diminished, and as a result, the OU

OKLAHOMA

OU PLAYERS IN THE COLLEGE FOOTBALL HALL OF FAME

Name	Pos.	Years	Inducted
Claude Reeds	FB	1910–1913	1961
Forest Geyer	FB	1913–1915	1973
Billy Vessels	HB	1950–1952	1974
Jim Owens	E	1946–1949	1982
Tommy McDonald	HB	1954–1956	1985
Waddy Young	E	1936–1938	1986
Lee Roy Selmon	DT	1972–1975	1988
Steve Owens	HB	1967–1969	1991
Jim Weatherall	T	1948–1951	1992
J.D. Roberts	G	1951–1953	1993
Billy Sims	HB	1975–1979	1995
Jerry Tubbs	C	1954–1956	1996
Greg Pruitt	HB	1970–1972	1999
Kurt Burris	C	1951–1954	2000
Keith Jackson	TE	1984–1987	2001
Tony Casillas	NG	1982–1985	2004
Joe Washington	RB	1972–1975	2005
Tom Brahaney	C	1970–1972	2007
Clendon Thomas	RB	1955–1957	2011

offense had sputtered. But during those weeks, the Sooners had been saving a play that would puncture the blitz-happy Longhorns: the sprint draw. The Sooners had become smitten with the sprint draw after facing it earlier against Alabama. "We were saving it for [Texas]," said Mike Stoops, OU's defensive coordinator.

By uncorking Griffin from the sprint draw, the second-ranked Sooners confused the third-ranked Horns early, then wore them down late. OU piled up 125 rushing yards in the first quarter, then 132 in the fourth. All told, on 32 carries, Griffin racked up a career-high 248 yards—the second-highest OU rushing total in the history of the rivalry. He also came up with the play of the game. Trailing 17–14 two minutes into the fourth quarter, OU faced third-and-goal at the Texas 6. Quarterback Nate Hybl hit wide receiver Will Peoples near the goal line, but Peoples coughed up the ball after taking a vicious hit. The ball popped out onto the grass at the 2, but Griffin scooped it up and hopped into the end zone. The Sooners never trailed again and won 35–24, leaving UT quarterback Chris Simms 0–3 against the Sooners. After the game, Simms was asked about his Cotton Bowl struggles. But before he could answer, Mack Brown intervened. "Let me answer that question," Brown said. "Chris is one of the best quarterbacks in the country."

That day, Stoops also spoke for Griffin, who did his best to dodge any opportunity to discuss himself. "Quentin is very special," Stoops said. "He loves to play in the Cotton Bowl." Griffin's career in the Cotton Bowl included 362 yards rushing, an average of 5.1 yards per carry, and nine touchdowns. If only he cared about that.

STEVE DAVIS

Steve Davis didn't look the part of a future star the first time he took the field at the Cotton Bowl. As a nervous freshman warming up in 1972, Davis overthrew a 15-yard out route so badly he hit a lady sitting in the stands and knocked her hat off. Just then Barry Switzer walked by and muttered, "Davis, you're gonna have to get a helluva lot better to ever play in this game."

Davis got better. Much better. And he would go on to quarterback the Sooners to a pair of national championships and a 3–0 record against the Longhorns. "Nobody thought Steve would ever play quarterback at OU," said Davis' favorite wide receiver, Tinker Owens. "But he's a big reason why we won a lot of football games."

As a kid growing up in the eastern Oklahoma town of Sallisaw, Davis had two dreams: to be a Baptist minister and quarterback the Sooners. "When I got out of high school, I only knew two songs: 'Boomer Sooner' and 'Amazing Grace,'" said Davis, who became an ordained Baptist minister as a teen. Davis idolized OU quarterback Bobby Warmack and did everything to look like him. But at first, the Sooners didn't want Davis and initially passed on offering him a scholarship. Davis wasn't big, wasn't particularly fast, and didn't have the strongest of arms. But close to signing day, a scholarship opened up after a previous commitment switched to Colorado. Assistant coach Leon Cross, who had been following Davis, convinced Switzer to offer him OU's final scholarship. "All he did was win," Cross said. "Every time he got under center, they did things right."

From left, OU quarterback Steve Davis, coach Barry Switzer, and running back Joe Washington give the "No. 1" sign in Miami Beach on January 2, 1976, after the AP named the Sooners national champions for the second year in a row.

When Davis got to Norman, he was eighth-string out of eight quarterbacks, with virtually no chance of ever playing, much less starting. "Back then, with the scholarship limits what they were, OU could take what they considered to be a marginal guy," Owens said. "If scholarships had been limited the way they are today, guys like me and Steve wouldn't have been at OU." Good thing for the Sooners they were. Over the course

of two years, Davis gradually ascended the depth chart. He couldn't throw like Warmack or run like Jack Mildren. But he had the unique knack for never screwing up. And with OU overflowing with talent on both sides of the ball, that's pretty much what the Sooners needed out of their quarterback. "He didn't beat us," Switzer said. "He was sound. That's why he played."

Davis was more than just sound against the Longhorns. In his Red River debut in '73, he passed for two touchdowns and ran for two more, as OU thrashed the Horns 52–13. The following year, he rushed for a 22-yard touchdown in the Sooners' 16–13 victory.

Then in '75 Davis called a brilliant audible late in the game, which led to Horace Ivory's go-ahead, 33-yard touchdown. "Steve's greatest asset was that he knew the mechanics of the wishbone," said split end Billy Brooks, who also reeled in a 54-yard bomb from Davis that game to set up OU's second touchdown. "He knew when to pitch the ball, when to keep it. Steve made the most of his ability, which is something that takes a lot of conviction."

Davis left OU as the winningest quarterback in school history with a 32–1–1 record as a starter. He was named Offensive MVP of the '75 Orange Bowl victory over Michigan, which sealed the Sooners' second consecutive national championship. "We never had to worry about the quarterback position," said halfback Joe Washington. "And when you don't have to worry about the quarterback position, that's a big deal."

4

GAMES OUR ANCESTORS LOVED

1905: OKLAHOMA 2, TEXAS 0

In 1905 a reserved young coach from Bethany College in Lindsborg, Kansas, accepted a three-month contract at Oklahoma for a total of $900. It turned out to be the bargain of the century for the burgeoning school.

In his first season, Bennie Owen led the "Boomers" to a 7–2 record, which included the program's first victory over Texas. In the final moments of the fourth quarter, and the game scoreless in Oklahoma City, OU's Bob Severin blasted through the Texas line, rammed into Don Robinson's knees, then carried Robinson across the goal line for a safety.

The Longhorns claimed that Severin was offside, but the referee saw it otherwise. Legend has it that immediately after the safety, fans charged the field and carried the Boomer players off the grounds, effectively ending the game with still a minute to play. The *Austin American-Statesman* pouted in an editorial the following day: "The result of this game may be that Texas will hereafter refuse to play these small colleges unless

it be here or at some place where all arrangements can be made beforehand to eradicate any such foolish performances as were tolerated at Oklahoma."

Owen went on to win seven more times against the Steers to finish with an 8–8 record in the series. Even after losing his right arm in a hunting accident, Owen continued coaching and retired after the 1926 season with a career record of 122–54–16. Today, the Sooners still play on "Owen Field."

1908: OKLAHOMA 50, TEXAS 0

Shortly after arriving in Oklahoma City via train, Texas captain L.H. Feldhake declared to the *Daily Oklahoman*, "There is every indication that we will win in tomorrow's contest with the Oklahoma 11." Bennie Owen knew better, countering, "We have a team that is the equal of the Texas team, and, if I judge correctly, much better. I predict a notable victory."

On one of the coldest days in Norman in years, the Sooners steamrolled the Steers. Charley Wantland returned a punt 90 yards for a touchdown, which ignited the 50–0 rout. Ralph Campbell and Willard Douglas led the charge. Douglas gained 220 yards, Campbell 181.

Despite the cold, Professor D.W. Ohern, head of the geology department, led 300 men on a "snake dance" across Boyd Field during halftime. Mercifully, the game was called with seven minutes left because of darkness, and Texas coach W.E. Metzenthin wasn't about to protest. Darkness, however, couldn't call the party. After the game, students gathered at

the library and, carrying torches, paraded around Norman into the night.

1910: OKLAHOMA 3, TEXAS 0

Freshman fullback Claude Reeds set two college football records this Thanksgiving Day. One for longest punt. One for shortest punt. As a result, the Sooners won because of Reeds. And almost lost because of him, too.

On the first drive of the game, the Longhorns looked like they were going to make it a long day for the visiting team. Texas went right down the field, but the Sooners made a valiant goal-line stand at the 1-yard line.

From there, the game turned into a punting war; after Reeds' first punt, that kind of game did not appear to favor the Boomers. Reeds badly shanked the kick, which traveled out of bounds at the Sooners 5, putting Texas back in striking distance. Yet once again, OU turned back the Steers.

The game went back and forth until the third quarter, when the Sooners caught a break. End Jimmy Rogers broke through the Texas ranks, popped the ball loose and recovered the fumble. The play set up Fred Capshaw's 37-yard field goal for the only points of the day.

Texas wouldn't go away easy, though. The Longhorns came right back, putting together another impressive drive. But for yet a third time, the OU defense bowed up. After the Longhorns made a first down inside the 1-yard line, OU guard Bob Wood dropped a Texas ball carrier for a loss. Then, on the next

play, Capshaw leaped the line and forced Texas quarterback Arnold Kirkpatrick to fumble. The Sooners recovered and immediately lined up for a punt. This time, Reeds kicked his way into Sooners lore. With Texas selling out to block the punt, Reeds booted the ball well over the return man, Kirkpatrick.

RED RIVER STREAKS OU FANS LOVE

Since 1948, OU vs. Texas has been a virtual draw. Thirty-one wins for the Sooners. Thirty wins for the Longhorns. And three ties. But for whatever reason, the series has always run in streaks. The streaks OU fans loved:

1948–1957: OU GOES 9–1

After eight straight losses, OU gains superiority of the series in 1948. Propelled by hard-nosed fullback Leon Heath, the Sooners prevail 20–14, helping launch the Wilkinson dynasty of the 1950s.

The 1953 win over Texas underscores the magic Sooner Nation enjoys in the 1950s. Korean War veteran Tom Carroll, making his first start, intercepts a Texas pitchout to set up OU's first touchdown, then runs 48 yards for the Sooners' last score, keying a 19–14 victory that was the first of OU's 47 straight wins, which includes five wins over the Longhorns.

1971–1975: OU GOES 5–0

Texas invents the wishbone, but the Sooners under Barry Switzer go on to perfect it. In 1971, with quarterback Jack Mildren pulling the triggers, OU's wishbone vanquishes Texas 48–27—a 53-point turnaround from its debut the year before.

The landmark win, however, comes in 1975, with OU ranked second and the Longhorns fifth. The battle goes back and forth until Horace Ivory's 33-yard touchdown run with 5:31 left caps a 79-yard, seven-

OKLAHOMA

The ball rolled all the way to the Texas 2 for a 107-yard punt. The Longhorns managed once again to drive into field-goal range, but the game ended with Kirkpatrick banging a field-goal try off the goal post, giving the Sooners their first series win in Texas. The Sooners had been 0–6–1 in Austin.

play drive that breaks a 17–17 tie and gives OU its 25th straight win and fifth in a row over Texas. The Sooners go on to win their fifth national championship.

1985–1988: OU GOES 4–0

In the mid-1980s, the Sooners return to their dominant defensive ways. Led by brash linebacker Brian Bosworth, OU obliterates the Texas offense.

Playing without superstar nose guard Tony Casillas in 1985, OU still holds Texas to just 70 total yards and four first downs, and Patrick Collins breaks a 7–7 tie with a 45-yard run with 12:25 left in the game to give the Sooners a bruising 14–7 win.

The next season, Bosworth predicts a 63–0 rout. He's not far off. OU leads 38–0 five minutes into the second half and coasts 47–12.

2000–2004: OU GOES 5–0

After a decade of relative mediocrity, OU turns the tables on Texas under Bob Stoops. The Sooners hammer Texas 63–14 in 2000 and 65–13 in 2003 in the two most lopsided margins in the series in the modern era.

The most memorable moment, though, comes in the closest game in 2001. With Texas pinned near its own goal line, Roy Williams sails over the offensive line and collides with quarterback Chris Simms. The hit jars the ball loose, and linebacker Teddy Lehman intercepts it and steps into the end zone to seal the 14–3 victory. Williams earns the nickname "Superman."

OKLAHOMA

Hundreds of students met the train that brought the Sooners back to Norman and, grasping the tongue of the train with their own hands, pulled it along Main Street while the band played. In front of Barbour's Drug Store, Owen and some of the players made short speeches.

Reeds, meanwhile, would go on to become OU's first All-American in 1913 and, in 1961, became the first Sooners player to be enshrined in the College Football Hall of Fame.

1915: OKLAHOMA 14, TEXAS 13

OU entered the 1915 season with its finest team under Bennie Owen. In their first four games, the Sooners outscored their opponents 248–0. But Texas was stout, as well. The Longhorns had outscored their first three opponents 223–0.

The game drew significant anticipation, and 12,000 fans showed up in Dallas' State Fair Park, the largest crowd to see a football game in Texas up to that point. For the first time, the OU band traveled to an away game, courtesy of two impromptu campus dances charging 10¢ a head sponsored by the cheerleaders and a new football support group called the "RUF/NEKS."

Uncharacteristic of the era, both OU and Texas were adept with the forward pass. But, as the *Daily Oklahoman* reported the following day, "Sooner grit, Sooner strategy, and Sooner endurance triumphed over Longhorn confidence, Longhorn beef, and Longhorn prayers." Longhorn beef, however, controlled the game early. On the opening kickoff, two Texas players collided with Spot Geyer, forcing a fumble the Horns

recovered. Three running plays later, Texas was in the end zone. OU countered to tie the game with a Hap Johnson touchdown catch, but in the third quarter, the Longhorns regained the lead on a five-yard touchdown run by Bob Simmons. Under the rules of the day, conversions came from the spot where the touchdown was scored. And Texas misfired on the extra point, which would be its eventual downfall.

With three minutes to play in the game, Geyer, who threw for 232 yards—130 in the fourth quarter alone—connected with Johnson for a 20-yard touchdown. From a difficult angle, Geyer also kicked the winning extra point, propelling the Sooners to the 14–13 victory. A huge crowd of 4,000 celebrated the win on Boyd Field the following Monday, enjoying barbecued steer and ice cream. The Sooners went on to go 10–0, their best record until Bud Wilkinson guided OU to an 11–0 finish 34 years later.

1933: OKLAHOMA 9, TEXAS 0

After Bennie Owen retired in 1926, the Sooners enjoyed little success against Texas. In fact, OU enjoyed little success against anyone. The week before the 1933 Red River tilt, the Sooners were trounced by Tulsa 20–6.

On a muddy field in Dallas, the OU offense had another modest afternoon and gained just 99 yards total with only four first downs. But in the trenches, the Sooners defensive linemen tossed their weight around. "In this soul-stirring gridiron drama, the OU linemen from end to end outcharged the Texas front ranks, rushed the passer, caused the passer back to throw 'em away, dropped the Texas ball carrier behind the line

OKLAHOMA

OU WINS OVER THE LONGHORNS

1905: OU 2, Texas 0

1908: OU 50, Texas 0

1910: OU 3, Texas 0

1911: OU 6, Texas 3

1912: OU 21, Texas 6

1915: OU 14, Texas 13

1917: OU 14, Texas 0

1919: OU 12, Texas 7

1933: OU 9, Texas 0

1938: No. 14 OU 13, Texas 0

1939: No. 3 OU 24, Texas 12

1948: No. 16 OU 20, Texas 14

1949: No. 3 OU 20, No. 12 Texas 14

1950: No. 3 OU 14, No. 4 Texas 13

1952: No. 12 OU 49, Texas 20

1953: No. 16 OU 19, No. 15 Texas 14

1954: No. 1 OU 14, No. 15 Texas 7

1955: No. 3 OU 20, Texas 0

1956: No. 1 OU 45, Texas 0

1957: No. 1 OU 21, Texas 7

1966: OU 18, Texas 9

1971: No. 4 OU 48, No. 3 Texas 27

1972: No. 2 OU 27, No. 10 Texas 0

1973: No. 6 OU 52, No. 13 Texas 13

1974: No. 2 OU 16, No. 17 Texas 13

1975: No. 2 OU 24, No. 5 Texas 17

1978: No. 1 OU 31, No. 6 Texas 10

1982: OU 28, No. 13 Texas 22

1985: No. 2 OU 14, No. 7 Texas 7

1986: No. 6 OU 47, Texas 12

1987: No. 1 OU 44, Texas 9

1988: No. 10 OU 28, Texas 13

1993: No. 10 OU 38, Texas 17

1996: OU 30, No. 25 Texas 27 (OT)

2000: No. 10 OU 63, No. 11 Texas 14

2001: No. 3 OU 14, No. 5 Texas 3

2002: No. 2 OU 35, No. 3 Texas 24

2003: No. 1 OU 65, No. 11 Texas 13

2004: No. 2 OU 12, No. 5 Texas 0

2007: No. 10 OU 28, No. 19 Texas 21

2010: No. 8 OU 28, No. 21 Texas 20

2011: No. 3 OU 55, No. 11 Texas 17

of scrimmage repeatedly, got down the field like greyhounds under punts," wrote *Daily Oklahoman* sports editor Bus Ham.

The Sooners capitalized off a pair of Texas mistakes on special teams for the only points of the game. OU end Jack

Harris sacked Buster Baebel for a 16-yard loss to the Longhorns 12-yard line. On the next play, Carlos Bell snapped the ball over punter Jimmy Hadlock's head for a safety. Then in the second half, Jeff Coker forced Hadlock to pull the ball in on a punt, and Owen Cason stripped him of the ball and recovered the fumble at Texas 8-yard line. Bob Dunlap raced around the right end and shot over the goal line, sending the OU crowd into a frenzy.

"So delirious were the spectators that many a nose-bleeding or eye-blacking fight cropped out here and there," Ham wrote. "But the Sooners down there on the battlefield of this sunken saucer, sweltering in summer heat, didn't let up; didn't lose their heads."

OU held on 9–0 for its only victory over Texas between 1919 and 1938.

5

TRADITIONS WE LOVE

SOONER MAGIC

In the decade between 1976 and 1986, Nebraska seemingly would always have Oklahoma beat, only to witness "Sooner Magic" lift OU to yet another improbable victory.

In 1976 OU trailed Nebraska 17–13 with only a couple of minutes to play and the ball deep in its own territory. Earlier, Barry Switzer had asked defensive back and team captain Scott Hill to deliver the pregame prayer. "Please, dear Lord, don't let any injury or harm come to any player," Hill prayed. "And please, please, please, dear Lord, please don't let the best team win."

"I knew we were going to need some help," Hill said. Help arrived in the form of Sooner Magic. Woodie Shepard completed a 47-yard halfback pass to freshman split end Steve Rhodes against double coverage. Two plays later, Rhodes ran a curl pattern, then pitched to halfback Elvis Peacock on the hook-and-ladder for another huge gain. Peacock scored the winning touchdown on next play with 38 seconds to go, catapulting the Sooners into a three-way tie for the conference championship.

DID YOU KNOW?

When Edwin Simmons arrived at Texas in 1983, some considered him the best freshman running back in the nation. In his collegiate debut, he torched the Sooners with two dazzling touchdown runs while overshadowing Marcus Dupree in the Longhorns' victory.

But the fall of his senior year, Simmons showed up five pounds overweight and explained that it was because he had been in summer school and had studied so hard his brain had taken on weight. Then the week of the OU game, he got arrested behind a house in Austin. A screen had been removed from one of the windows. According to police, Simmons had trouble coming up with his name or what town he was in. He did say, however, "I think I'm a football player.... I think my number is 33." Oh, and Simmons was nude.

The Sooners got their jabs in. Barry Switzer congratulated a reporter on asking a question and said, "You get the prize. And the prize is Edwin Simmons' clothes."

Quarterback Jamelle Holieway added, "We don't do that here. Coach Switzer does not encourage us to run around with our pants down."

OKLAHOMA

A decade later, Sooner Magic struck Lincoln again. A Jamelle Holieway fumble seemingly had handed Nebraska the game-clinching turnover. Instead, the Huskers were flagged with a face-mask penalty, giving OU new life. With 1:22 remaining, Holieway found tight end Keith Jackson, who ripped the ball away from a Nebraska defensive back for a game-tying touchdown. The game was headed for a 17–17 tie. Or so it seemed. After Nebraska punted, OU had the ball on its side of the field with only 18 seconds left. But on third-and-12, Holieway heaved a pass down the sideline, and Jackson hauled it in with one hand before racing 41 yards down the sideline. OU kicked

the game-winning field goal on the next play to seal another trip to the Orange Bowl. "Nebraska believed we'd do it," Switzer said afterward, "and we did."

BOOMER SOONER

Most people believe that Oklahoma's fight song comes from Yale University's "Boola Boola." But the roots of "Boomer Sooner" actually go back further, derived from a song telling of Boston girls who will treat you nice if you have money, and Philadelphia girls that will call you honey, apparently irrespective of your net worth.

Arthur Alden, an OU history and physiology student, whose father was a Norman jeweler, wrote "Boomer Sooner" in 1905. Alden set the lyrics to the tune of "Boola Boola."

Over the years, Yale students and others have accused OU of lifting their fight song. Truth is, Yale stole the tune from someone else. Allan Hirsh is credited with composing "Boola Boola" in 1900—a day before he and his fellow students belted the ballad as the Bulldogs beat rival Harvard 28–0. It's been proven, however, that the song owes a substantial debt to an 1898 song by the name of "La Hoola Boola," which was written by African American songwriters Robert Allen "Bob" Cole and Billy Johnson.

Anyway, a year after Alden wrote "Boomer Sooner," the ending was added from North Carolina's "I'm a Tarheel Born," placing the finishing touches on what has become one of the most recognizable fight songs in all of college football.

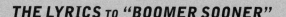

THE LYRICS *TO* "BOOMER SOONER"

Boomer Sooner, Boomer Sooner
Boomer Sooner, Boomer Sooner
Boomer Sooner, Boomer Sooner
Boomer Sooner, OK U!

Oklahoma, Oklahoma
Oklahoma, Oklahoma
Oklahoma, Oklahoma
Oklahoma, OK U!

I'm a Sooner born and Sooner bred
and when I die, I'll be Sooner dead
Rah Oklahoma, Rah Oklahoma
Rah Oklahoma, OK U!

OKLAHOMA

MEX

Before "Top Daug," there was a dog named "Mex."

In 1914 during the Mexican Revolution, Mott Keys, an Army hospital medic stationed along the border near Laredo, Texas, stumbled onto Mex among a litter of abandoned terrier puppies south of the border. Keys' company adopted Mex, and Keys took the dog back to Hollis, Oklahoma, after completing his duty. When Keys enrolled at the University of Oklahoma, Mex enrolled, too.

Keys' experience as an Army medic landed him a job working for the OU football team. Mex would go to the games,

OKLAHOMA

OKLAHOMA COACHES IN THE COLLEGE FOOTBALL HALL OF FAME

Name	OU Coach	Inducted
Bennie Owen	1905–1926	1951
Biff Jones	1935–1936	1954
Bud Wilkinson	1947–1963	1969
Jim Tatum	1946	1984
Barry Switzer	1973–1988	2001

donning a red sweater with a big red letter *O* on the side and barking whenever the Sooners scored a touchdown. Mex also was charged with keeping stray dogs and cats from roaming onto Boyd Field in the middle of games.

But it wasn't until a football road trip to Drake in 1924 that Mex truly became famous. When the Sooners switched trains in Arkansas City, Kansas, to head for Des Moines, Iowa, Mex did not switch with them. Without their mascot, the Sooners were tattooed by Drake 28–0. A headline in the *Arkansas Daily Traveler* said it all: "Crushing Defeat of Bennie Owen's Team is Charged to Loss of Their Mascot Here." A 50¢ reward was offered to whoever could locate OU's mascot. Mex was eventually discovered in Arkansas City, pacing the train station platform. OU alums J.D. Hull, Hughes B. Davis, and J.C. Henley recovered the dog and drove him to OU's next game in Stillwater against Oklahoma A&M. Mex didn't bring the Sooners any more luck, though. OU lost again, 6–0.

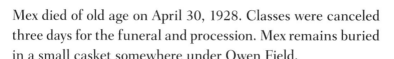

Mex died of old age on April 30, 1928. Classes were canceled three days for the funeral and procession. Mex remains buried in a small casket somewhere under Owen Field.

THE SOONER SCHOONER

The Sooner Schooner was introduced to OU football games during the 1964 season and became an official school mascot in 1980. The Schooner, a conestoga, or covered wagon, was a replica of the prairie wagons used by those who settled Oklahoma during the Land Run of 1889. The original Shetland ponies to pull the Schooner were called "Mike" and "Ike," named after the candy. These days, the ponies go by "Boomer" and "Sooner."

Whenever the Sooners score, the ponies take the wagon on a lap around one side of the field during home games. With the way the Sooners have scored some seasons at Owen Field, that can be one arduous task. In 2003 OU called off the wagon

DID YOU KNOW?

In the 1940s Bud Wilkinson unearthed his future quarterback in the most unlikely of places.

Claude Arnold had just returned from the service and decided to join the Delta Tau Delta fraternity instead of the football team. "Our intramural touch football team was pretty dominant," Arnold said. "We beat everybody, and I was pretty much the whole team."

Wilkinson took notice and, before the 1948 season, persuaded Arnold to go out for football with the promise of a scholarship. Arnold agreed and would help quarterback the Sooners to wins over the Longhorns in '48, '49, and '50.

OKLAHOMA

The Sooner Schooner is driven onto the field after a touchdown in the second quarter of Oklahoma's 26–6 win over Iowa State in 2011.

after its third touchdown against Texas A&M, in part due to damp conditions. That turned out to be a wise decision. The Sooners would score eight more touchdowns to humiliate the Aggies 77–0.

Of course, like any mascot, the Sooner Schooner has endured its share of controversial moments. During the 1984 season, OU entered the Orange Bowl against Washington, ranked

second in the country and still with a shot at capturing the national championship over top-ranked Brigham Young.

The game was tied 14–14 early in the fourth quarter, when Tim Lashar's 22-yard field goal appeared to give the Sooners the lead. Problem was, OU had been penalized for illegal procedure on the attempt. Tackle Mark Hutson, wearing a tight end number for special offensive packages, failed to report his jersey number to the officiating crew before lining up, resulting in a five-yard penalty.

Those riding the Schooner, however, never saw the flag and came riding onto the field. What's more, the wagon stalled in front of Washington's bench, making it look like the Schooner was taunting the Huskies. Officials flagged the Sooners again, this time for a delay of game/unsportsmanlike 15-yard penalty on the Schooner. Lashar's second kick from 42 yards was blocked, and the Huskies went on to a 28–17 victory, handing BYU the national title. "I'm upset," Barry Switzer said during a live TV interview after the game. "The officials shouldn't allow that to happen in the ballgame."

Eight years after the "Sooner Schooner Game," the wagon made headlines again for the wrong reasons. In the middle of a 27–10 loss to Colorado, the Schooner made too sharp a turn and tumbled over to its left, tossing driver Scott Gibson, flag-waver Ryan Wray, and the RUF/NEK queen, Jean Connelly, who was riding shotgun, to the turf. Gibson suffered a broken arm, but most of the crowd's attention was directed at the queen, whose skirt flew up during the fall. She was not wearing any underwear.

OKLAHOMA

CONFERENCE CHAMPIONSHIPS (43)

Big 12 Conference
2010, 2008, 2007, 2006, 2004, 2002, 2000 (Bob Stoops)
Big 8 Conference
1987, 1986, 1985, 1984, 1980, 1979, 1978, 1977, 1976, 1975, 1974,
1973 (Barry Switzer)
1972, 1968, 1967 (Chuck Fairbanks)
1962 (Bud Wilkinson)
Big 7 Conference
1959, 1958, 1957, 1956, 1955, 1954, 1953, 1952, 1951, 1950, 1949,
1948 (Bud Wilkinson)
Big 6 Conference
1947 (Bud Wilkinson)
1946 (Jim Tatum)
1944, 1943 (Snorter Luster)
1938 (Tom Stidham)
Missouri Valley Conference
1920 (Bennie Owen)
Southwest Conference
1918, 1915 (Bennie Owen)

OKLAHOMA!

Oklahoma remains the only state to adopt its official song from a Broadway musical.

Oklahoma! opened in March 1943 and was an immediate box-office smash, running for an unprecedented 2,243 performances. In 1955 the Richard Rodgers and Oscar Hammerstein production was adapted into a film, and captured several Academy Awards. Not only was *Oklahoma!* a success on Broadway and film, it helped restore pride to a state that was decimated

by the Dust Bowl in the 1930s. Before every home game—and at the Cotton Bowl—the Pride of Oklahoma takes the field to "Fanfare & Oklahoma." As the band booms "Oklahoma!" the drum major struts down the field with his head tipped back while a giant state of Oklahoma flag is unveiled.

THE RUF/NEKS

At an Oklahoma–Oklahoma A&M basketball game in 1915, a group of football players were cheering obnoxiously, irritating an elderly woman behind them. She eventually hollered at them, "Sit down and be quiet, you roughnecks!"

THE LYRICS TO "OKLAHOMA!"

Oklahoma, where the wind comes sweepin' down the plain
And the wavin' wheat can sure smell sweet
When the wind comes right behind the rain.

Oklahoma, Ev'ry night my honey lamb and I
Sit alone and talk and watch a hawk
Makin' lazy circles in the sky.

We know we belong to the land
And the land we belong to is grand!

And when we say:
Ee-ee-ow! A-yip-i-o-ee-ay!
We're only sayin',
You're doin' fine, Oklahoma!
Oklahoma, O-K!

OKLAHOMA

SOONERS BOOKS WE LOVE

Oklahoma Kickoff by Harold Keith

Bootlegger's Boy
by Barry Switzer with Bud Shrake

Forty-Seven Straight: The Wilkinson Era at Oklahoma by Harold Keith and Berry Tramel

Presidents Can't Punt by George Lynn Cross

The Oklahoma Football Vault
by Kenny Mossman

Bud Wilkinson: An Intimate Portrait of an American Legend by Jay Wilkinson

Sooner Century by Brent Clark

The Undefeated by Jim Dent

Tales From the Sooner Sidelines
by Jay C. Upchurch

The Oklahoma Football Encyclopedia
by Ray Dozier

The name stuck. And the RUF/NEKS have been synonymous with OU football ever since. The all-male sprit group carries around red-and-white paddles and fires shotguns, which had the original purpose of intimidating visiting opponents.

The University of Texas became so exasperated by the shot-gun blasts of the RUF/NEKS after OU touchdowns, the school commissioned its engineering department in 1953 to construct a response in the form of "Smokey the Cannon." But the cannon couldn't save the Longhorns on the field. OU prevailed 19–14 over the Horns in '53, the first win in the school's 47-game winning streak.

After the victory, the RUF/NEKS led the charge of tear-ing down the Cotton Bowl's wooden goal posts. Coach Bud Wilkinson's oldest son, Pat, still just a kid, was on the sideline and tried to join in. But a RUF/NEK standing nearby, annoyed a kid was trying to steal a piece of the goal post, swatted him in the head with part of the wood, temporarily knocking him out. After being told the tale later, Wilkinson couldn't stifle a chuckle.

O.K. OKLAHOMA

Fred Waring, who created the Waring Blender and who first made smoothies trendy to drink, was also a renowned bandleader of the 1930s. He had a radio show on NBC called *The Chesterfield Hour* and would often compose new fight songs for universities. In 1939 the students at OU petitioned him to write a new fight song for the Sooners, and War-ing responded by composing the music and lyrics of "O.K. Oklahoma."

Ironically, the first verse bearing the song's title eventually fell out of the current arrangement. Even so, "O.K. Oklahoma" has been part of every OU football game, as the Pride of Okla-homa plays the tune after the Sooners score an extra point.

THE CRIMSON AND CREAM

Before the turn of the 20th century, the two most popular pastimes on OU's campus were football and oratory. In the fall of 1895, the combination of OU's first football game and first oratory contest prompted university leaders to create an official set of school colors to be flaunted at these events. May Overstreet, an English instructor and the first woman on the faculty, was appointed to chair a committee along with Dr. James Buchanan to select the colors.

OKLAHOMA

THE LYRICS *TO* "O.K. OKLAHOMA"

O.K. Oklahoma, K.O. the foe today.
We say O.K. Oklahoma, the Sooners know the way. 'Ray!
S double-O N-E-R-S! We'll win today or miss our guess.
O.K. Oklahoma, K.O. the foe today.

We'll march down the field with our heads held high,
Determined to win any battle we're in,
We'll fight with all our might for the Red and White.
March on, march on down the field for a victory is nigh.
You know we came to win the game for Oklahoma,
And so we will or know the reason why!

We'll march down the field with our heads held high,
With ev'ry resource we'll hold to the course,
And pledge our heart and soul to reach the goal.

March on, march on down the field as we sing the battle cry.
Dig in and fight for the Red and White of Oklahoma,
So we'll take home a victory or die!

The committee initially recommended "crimson" and "corn." But local merchants had difficulty determining the color of corn for merchandise, and so the committee revised its suggestion to crimson and "cream." The student body and the merchants ratified the nomination, and almost overnight, they transformed the campus with crimson-and-cream pennants, banners, and decorations, to the point the merchants couldn't keep up with the demand.

That year, the OU Oratorical Society donned the colors for the first time at a contest in Guthrie. And, before long, the football team would do the same.

THE OU CHANT

The Chant was written in 1936 by Jessie Lone Clarkson Gilkey, who directed the OU girls' glee club. The school loved the chant so much that Gilkey was voted OU's outstanding faculty woman the following year.

DID YOU KNOW?

Halfback Clendon Thomas scored three touchdowns in OU's 45–0 rout of the Longhorns in 1956. A remarkable feat considering he spent the previous night in the bathtub.

"I was in the infirmary the day before the game and I had the flu all week," said Thomas, who was also on medication all week. "I remember going to the tub, putting cold water in it, and just sitting there. Whatever it took to feel better."

OKLAHOMA

OKLAHOMA

NATIONAL CHAMPIONSHIP SEASONS

Year	Record	Coach
1950	10–1	Bud Wilkinson
1955	11–0	Bud Wilkinson
1956	10–0	Bud Wilkinson
1974	11–0	Barry Switzer
1975	11–1	Barry Switzer
1985	11–1	Barry Switzer
2000	13–0	Bob Stoops

Every student and alum stands and raises his or her index finger during the Chant:

> O-K-L-A-H-O-M-A
> *Our chant rolls on and on!*
> *Thousands strong*
> *Join heart and song*
> *In alma mater's praise*
> *Of campus beautiful by day and night*
> *Of colors proudly gleaming Red and White*
> *'Neath a western sky*
> *OU's chant will never die.*
> *Live on University!*

HORNS DOWN

At a 1955 pep rally, Texas cheerleader Harley Clark taught his fellow students the "Hook 'em Horns" hand signal to counter Texas A&M's "Gig 'Em" sign. Soon, Oklahoma fans coun-

tered with a sign of their own: the Horns Down. This can be a touchy issue with Texas fans—and former players. In 2010 former Texas quarterback Vince Young attacked a strip club manager after the manager flashed the Horns Down to Young's face.

Other non-OU fans have been known to throw the Horns Down sign, too. In the 2009 national championship, Alabama quarterback Greg McElroy flashed the sign following the Crimson Tide's second touchdown as he walked off the field.

I HATE TEXAS

JAKE TROTTER

TRIUMPH
BOOKS

CONTENTS

1

GAMES WE HATE

1984

TEXAS	7	3	0	5	**15**
OKLAHOMA	0	0	15	0	**15**

Years later, it's not the losses to Texas that gnaw at Barry Switzer. It's the ties. In 1976 the Sooners settled for a 6–6 tie after botching an extra point late in the fourth quarter. Eight years later, maybe the worst officiating call in the history of the series allowed the Longhorns to kick a game-tying field goal. "We were a young team in '76, but we were still a pretty good football team," Switzer said. "But we were ranked [No. 3] the day we played in '84. Now that game…it's hard to beat Texas. I've always been pissed off two of my ties should have been victories against Texas. Victories against Texas, they were hard to get."

The '76 Sooners proved to be a flawed team. They lost at home to Terry Miller and Oklahoma State and snuck into a three-way tie for the Big 8 title. The '84 Sooners, however, were as good as any team in the country. OU strolled into the Cotton Bowl undefeated. The Longhorns were No. 1. There would be no doubt left as to who was the better team. "We won that football game," said halfback Patrick Collins.

"We battled one of the best teams in the country and won the football game." Unfortunately for the Sooners, the scoreboard didn't show it.

Switzer wanted to beat Texas so badly that season he wore a special hat to prove it. On the front of the cap given to him by a manager was an oval patch normally reserved for the name of a gas company. Instead, the words "Beat Texas" had been pinned there. Switzer can't recall exactly where he got the hat from, but he does remember the rain cascading down his face all game. "I couldn't see," he said. "The damn water was in my eyes." It would seem as if the referees had water in their eyes, too.

With a downpour affecting conditions, the Longhorns took a 10-point lead into halftime—but only because the Sooners handed those points to them. OU punter Mike Winchester had a snap slip through his hands, giving Texas the ball at the Sooners 26. Three plays later, Todd Dodge found Bill Boy Bryant for a 25-yard touchdown.

In the second quarter, Sooners quarterback Danny Bradley pitched a fumble the Longhorns recovered, again at the OU 26. But this time, linebacker Brian Bosworth and nose guard Tony Casillas stuffed the Horns and forced a field goal. "Our defense completely dominated the game," Switzer would say afterward. "We were behind 10–0, and our defense had not given up a first down. We felt like our defense could continue to stop them in the second half."

In the third quarter, the Sooners didn't just stop the Longhorns, they obliterated them. Bosworth drilled Texas running

back Terry Orr, and OU recovered the fumble at the Texas 6. Two plays later, Steve Sewell was in the end zone. On the next series, the Sooners defense stuffed Texas again, and the Long-horns had to punt from their own end zone. Instead Terry Steelhammer snapped the ball well over John Teltschik's head and through the back of the end zone.

At halftime, an OU offensive coordinator named Mack Brown made a key adjustment to go north and south in the rain instead of sideline-to-sideline. And on the next series that adjustment would pay off, with Spencer Tillman and Sewell slicing through the Texas defense. Sewell finished off the drive by bouncing off tackle for an 12-yard score to give OU the 15–10 lead after a failed two-point try.

Midway through the fourth quarter, the Longhorns finally got something on a bit of a fluke. Dodge handed off to Kevin Nelson, a freshman receiver who changed his number from 83 to 32 just before the game. The mystery tailback caught the Sooners off guard and dashed 58 yards to the OU 2. After getting clobbered all game, the Horns were primed to take back the lead. Instead, OU stuffed Texas on three straight runs, then threw Nelson for a loss on a sweep on fourth down. "We lined up in our 'Mad Dog' and went after them," Casillas said. "They tried to run the middle three times, and all of us were there. On fourth down, we expected them to fake inside and go outside. We were out there waiting for that, too."

With only a couple minutes remaining, Switzer was left with a difficult decision with the ball near his own goal line. Punt the ball out or take a safety. The Sooners had already committed a turnover on a punt, and a mistake here would give

TOP 5 TEXAS RUSHING GAMES vs. OU

1. **Ricky Williams** | 223 yards | 1997
   40 carries, 2 TDs | 27–24 (Texas)

2. **Hodges Mitchell** | 204 yards | 1999
   30 carries, TD | 38–28 (Texas)

3. **Jack Crain** | 144 yards | 1941
   10 carries, 2 TDs | 40–7 (Texas)

4. **Jack Crain** | 142 yards | 1939
   6 carries, 2 TDs | 24–12 (OU)

5. **Ricky Williams** | 139 yards | 1998
   31 carries, 2 TDs | 34–3 (Texas)

Texas the win. So Switzer gambled and took the safety, making the score 15–12. "I think it was a better play than to risk a punt from deep in the zone," he would explain afterward. "We weren't real sharp with our punting today. We wanted to be in safe position to put the ball in their end of the field, and that's exactly what we did. Texas hadn't moved the ball against us with a sustained drive all day. Naturally, I didn't think they would then, either."

Of course, Switzer wasn't counting on the Horns getting loads of help from the officials. On Texas' first snap, fullback Jerome Johnson coughed up the ball after being leveled by Sooners linebacker Paul Migliazzo. Casillas appeared to have recovered the ball, effectively ending the game. Instead, officials

ruled that Johnson had been down and gave Texas the ball back. "[The official] was adjusting his glasses when the ball pops out," Switzer said. "We clearly had the ball." Instead, Texas did. Two plays later on third-and-7, Dodge sailed a pass over the head of wideout Brent Duhon. Officials, however, called the Sooners for defensive interference even though the pass appeared to be uncatchable. "They blew that one," Switzer said. "We made a clean play on it."

But the worst was yet to come. With just a few seconds left on the clock, Dodge rolled right and threw a pass into the end zone for Bryant. Instead, OU cornerback Andre Johnson tipped the ball into the air and into the arms of a diving Keith Stanberry for the apparent game-ending interception. Stanberry swore he was in bounds, and the TV replays confirmed it. But officials ruled that Stanberry was out when he caught the ball. With one more play, Jeff Ward kicked a 32-yard field goal as time ran out to give the Longhorns a 15–15 tie. Switzer was livid after the game. So were his players. "We completely outplayed them," Bradley said.

The late calls tarnished what was one of the great defensive performances in Sooners history. Dodge, who came into the game second in the nation in passing, completed just six of 24 passes for 74 yards. Outside of Nelson's long run, the Horns gained just 38 yards on the ground. "The defense played up to everyone's expectations," Tillman would say. "They played a great game."

In the locker room, the mood was as if the Sooners had lost. "It was silent for 10 minutes," Bradley recalled. "No one said a word. Coach Switzer was standing there, too, thinking about

what had gone down. Then he looks up and says, 'You're the best team in the country. You just beat the No. 1 team in the country. Keep it together, and we'll win the national championship.'"

The Sooners went into their final game with a chance at accomplishing just that. But a loss to Washington in the Orange Bowl assured Brigham Young the national title.

1963

TEXAS	7	7	7	7	28
OKLAHOMA	0	0	7	0	7

In all his years, Bud Wilkinson recruited only one junior-college player to Oklahoma. He explicitly booted only one player, too. Turned out, they were one and the same.

After dominating college football in the 1950s, Wilkinson fell on hard times in the '60s. OU won only three games in 1960, and just five the following year. In those two seasons, Texas under Darrell Royal had drubbed the Sooners by a combined score of 52–7. Wilkinson had always valued discipline in his program and for the most part only recruited players he felt could meet that standard. But in 1962, desperate to get the program on the right track, Wilkinson relaxed his own standards and pursued a hotshot fullback with a checkered past residing at Cameron State in Lawton, Oklahoma.

Joe Don Looney's college career actually began at the University of Texas, though not on the gridiron. Looney, whose father, Don, had played with Davey O'Brien on TCU's 1938

national championship team, was never taken seriously as a high school football prospect. He once famously skipped out of a regional track meet after taking in too much pasta and beer for lunch. Looney attended UT just as a student, but flunked out after his first semester. He transferred to TCU with intentions to go out for the football team but never did. He was on his way to getting kicked out of TCU, too, when his father intervened and got him on the Cameron football team.

Looney had always been a physical marvel, with 6'1", 207-pound size and such blazing speed he could run the 100-yard dash in 9.6 seconds. Finally, those talents began to show on the football field. After leading Cameron to an undefeated season, schools like Tennessee and Wisconsin came calling. But after Wilkinson offered, Rooney signed with the Sooners.

Initially, the recruitment of Looney appeared to be a stroke of genius. In the 1962 opener, Wilkinson put Looney in with the Sooners trailing Syracuse 3–0 late in the game. "Just give me the ball, and I'll score a touchdown," Looney told Monte Deere, OU's quarterback. Deere did, and on his fourth career carry, Looney busted through the left side of the Orangemen front 60 yards for the game-winning touchdown. The media hailed Looney as the savior of Sooners football. Inside the locker room, he became something very different to the players. "He could be a real good guy, personable at times," said halfback Charles Mayhue. "But he was in it for himself. He was a pouter. He didn't like to practice and went to great lengths to get out of it." Rooney's go-to injury was a "stone bruise" on his foot, which at the time was neither detectable nor treatable. Looney finished the season fifth in the country in rushing and

first in punting and was named an All-American. But by the end of the season, his act was wearing thin with Wilkinson and the players. Looney skipped spring practice under the auspices he would run track. Instead, he claimed to pull a muscle and did almost no running. In the fall, Looney showed up for two-a-days out of shape and weighing 233 pounds, 26 more than his playing weight the season before.

In spite of Looney's off-field antics, Wilkinson had his best squad since the 47-game winning streak. After dominating Clemson and beating USC in Los Angeles, the Sooners were ranked No. 1. Texas, *Sports Illustrated*'s preseason pick to win the national championship, was No. 2, giving the series its first-ever No. 1 vs. No. 2 matchup.

That Sooners swagger, which had been missing for so many years, seemed to be back, too. After the USC game, OU tackle Ralph Neely looked into the CBS television camera and said, "Texas, you're next." In reality, the Sooners were a team about to come apart at the seams.

Looney had put together a fabulous performance in the 17–12 win over the then No. 1 Trojans. But moments before kickoff of the Clemson game, Looney told Wilkinson he couldn't play because he had felt a muscle twitch. Then, after the USC game, Looney complained that he had not been introduced as a starter on the CBS national telecast. Looney's disgruntlement continued to brew.

After USC, OU had two weeks to prepare for Texas, which meant extra conditioning and scrimmaging. Looney wanted no part of either. He sat out several practices, citing a stone

STREAKS OU FANS HATE: 1940–1947

Since 1940, OU vs. Texas has been a virtual draw—30 wins for the Sooners, 30 wins for the Longhorns, and three ties. But for whatever reason, the series has always run in streaks. The streaks we hated:

TEXAS GOES 8–0

After back-to-back losses in 1938 and 1939, the Longhorns return to dominating the series. After winning 19–16 in 1940, the Sooners fail to score more than 14 points once during their eight-game losing streak. The Horns, however, have help to pull off win eight.

After the first-half clock runs out in 1947, referee Jack Sisco rules from nowhere that Texas had called timeout. Allowed to run another play, Texas scores to take a lead into halftime. Sisco isn't done, either. In the second half, he waves off an OU interception by calling a penalty, and Texas scores on the drive to go up 28–14. Pandemonium ensues. Seat cushions and bottles are thrown onto the field, and after the game OU fans charge Sisco, who flees to the safety of a Texas Highway Patrol car.

TEXAS

bruise on his heel. In one of the practices he actually did participate in, Looney tried to punch graduate assistant John Tatum after the two got into a skirmish during a dummy blocking drill.

"Joe Don just wasn't giving any effort, he wasn't performing anywhere close to his ability," Mayhue said. "As a result, morale on the team wasn't very good."

That showed at the Cotton Bowl. In one of the most dominating defensive efforts in series history, Texas tackle Scott Apple-

ton and linebacker Tommy Nobis completely manhandled the OU offense. Appleton finished with 18 tackles and a fumble recovery that led to Texas' third touchdown, and Nobis killed a mild Sooners rally with an interception in the fourth quarter. Looney managed to rush for only six yards on four carries, as the Longhorns sailed to a 28–7 win. "They just kicked the shit out of us," Looney, who cockily declared before the game that he wouldn't "sweat" Texas, would say. "We weren't ready. We were too cocky."

In his newsletter, a dejected Wilkinson wrote that he could "never recall an Oklahoma team playing with as little fire and determination. When a team loses without preparing to the best of its ability and without playing with its greatest effort—particularly in a vitally important game—you cannot help but pause, reflect, and wonder why."

Wilkinson needed little time for reflection. On Monday, he called a meeting with the team's captains and informed them he was leaning toward kicking his All-America halfback off the team. By vote, the captains unanimously ratified the edict.

In an interview with the *Fort Worth Star-Telegram*, Looney's father claimed Wilkinson had called him and said that Joe Don "had lots of ability, but he had some bad practices last week, and we decided that this cost us the ballgame." Don Looney was incensed with Wilkinson and told the *Star-Telegram*, "Those people up there are not our kind of people, and I am glad Joe Don is through with them. I just wish this would have happened last week so I could have rooted for Texas."

With no more college eligibility, Looney entered the NFL Draft and was the 12th overall pick of the New York Giants. After only four weeks in camp, the Giants had enough, too, and traded Looney to the Colts, who traded him to the Lions, who shipped him to the Redskins. NFL Films later selected Looney as the "most uncoachable player" in NFL history.

With Looney no longer a distraction, OU bounced back to win six of its last seven games and finish 8–2. Wilkinson, however, retired after the season and ended his hall of fame career with six straight losses to the Longhorns.

2008

TEXAS	3	17	10	15	45
OKLAHOMA	7	14	7	7	35

The 2008 Red River Rivalry ended up being decided on two plays. The first convinced the Longhorns they could win. The second ensured that they would.

After installing the no-huddle offense in the off-season, Oklahoma came into the Cotton Bowl on a roll. The Sooners hung half a hundred on their first three opponents, then buried TCU and Baylor in contests that were never in doubt. Sophomore maestro Sam Bradford orchestrated the hurry-up flawlessly, as the Sooners rapidly climbed to No. 1 in the rankings. A couple of underlying flaws that were beginning to surface, however, would prove to be OU's undoing in Dallas.

After losing Limas Sweed, Jamaal Charles, and Jermichael Finley—its three best offensive playmakers—to the NFL

Colt McCoy, who holds almost every passing record at Texas, prepares to let fly against Oklahoma during the Longhorns' 45–35 comeback win over the No. 2–ranked Sooners in 2008.

Draft earlier in the year, Texas opened the season outside the top 10 in the polls. After quietly winning their first five games, however, the Longhorns were ranked fifth going into the game against the 5–0 Sooners. But the eyes of everyone were on Bradford and the Boomers, who were touchdown favorites.

The game began as most had expected it—with OU moving the ball at will. On their opening drive, the Sooners zipped eight plays down the field and put the ball in the end zone on Bradford's

five-yard strike to Manny Johnson. Three possessions later, Bradford and Ryan Broyles connected four times, the last an eight-yard touchdown pass. OU led 14–3 and smelled Bevo blood. "We were doing everything we wanted to on offense," said center Jon Cooper. "It felt like we were about to put them away."

That's when one of the Sooners' underlying flaws finally burned them. OU entered the Red River game ranked 104th in the nation in kickoff coverage. The Sooners had been so dominating through their first five games that it hadn't mattered. It would matter this time.

Off the ensuing kickoff, Texas' Jordan Shipley took the ball at the 4, found a gaping seam to the right, then sped untouched for a 96-yard touchdown. In a flash the game had become a game again. "It would have been pretty demoralizing for them to go down 21–3," Cooper said. "That play gave them confidence. They hadn't done anything on offense, and yet it was now just a four-point game. They're thinking, *We got a chance.* It gave them new life." The Sooners could have survived the Shipley kick return. But they could not survive the game's second turning point.

OU carried a 21–20 lead into halftime, then opened the third quarter the way it had the first. On the very first snap, tackle Gerald McCoy busted through the Texas line and sacked Colt McCoy for a big loss. The Horns punted after a three-and-out, and Bradford went back to work. He hit Johnson for 30 on a screen, then three plays later, Johnson again on the same screen play for a 14-yard touchdown. The drive took less than two minutes, and the Sooners were back in command, 28–20. That wouldn't last long.

On the first play of Texas' ensuing drive, OU middle line-backer Ryan Reynolds pursued a pitch to Chris Ogbonnaya to the right side of the field. As Reynolds closed to help with the tackle, Texas tackle Adam Ulatoski planted his helmet into Reynolds' knee. Reynolds tried to ignore the pain in his right knee and hobble back to the huddle. But, ultimately, the knee gave out. The anterior cruciate ligament had been severed.

Reynolds had already suffered two major knee injuries in his career, which had kept him from reaching his five-star poten-tial. But in '08 he was playing the best ball of his life. In fact, the week before in the win at Baylor, Reynolds became the first linebacker in the Bob Stoops era to grade out with a "100 percent" performance. "At that point in time, Ryan was the backbone of our defense," said fellow linebacker Keenan Clayton. "When he got hurt, the air just let out of everybody. You could see it later on the film. The whole demeanor of the defense changed. After that, it was all downhill."

Not only had OU lost the backbone of its defense, it had no viable or prepared replacement. With no better option, the Sooners subbed in Brandon Crow, who to that point had never made a tackle in his career. "Coach Venables liked keeping the ones in during practice the whole time, especially OU-Texas week," Reynolds said. "Brandon did the best he could, it was just one of those situations where he hadn't been shown the defense or gotten the repetitions."

This time, Texas smelled blood. Shrewdly, offensive coordi-nator Greg Davis slid Shipley to UT's flexed tight end slot in order to isolate him on Crow. With Crow unable to keep up, Shipley worked his way into the pockets and seams and gashed

the Sooners. Davis also exploited the Reynolds injury by running Ogbonnaya wide to the sidelines. More times than not, Crow took a poor angle and couldn't get to the corner in time or was knocked off his path. "Nothing bad on Crow. He wasn't ready, he was too young," Clayton said. "Once he got in the huddle, and Coach V was giving him the calls, his eyes were like this, just huge. Right there, I was like, *Oh no. Just calm down, man. Just calm down.* That was his first action. That's a big game to go in on your first game. That's crazy when you think about it."

Bradford, who finished with an OU-Texas record 387 yards passing and five touchdowns, tried to keep the Sooners in the game. But without Reynolds, the OU defense capitulated.

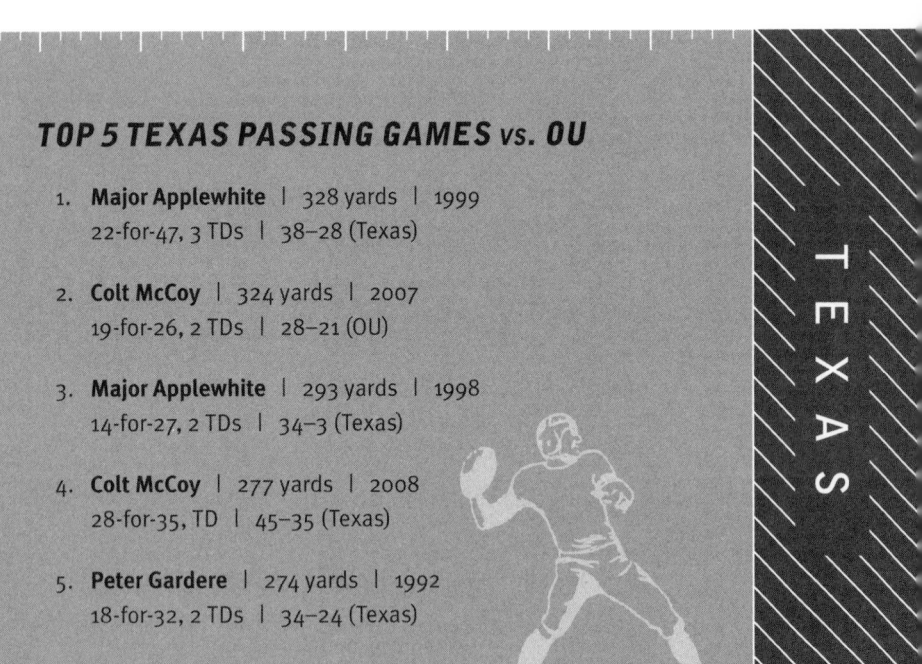

TOP 5 TEXAS PASSING GAMES vs. OU

1. **Major Applewhite** | 328 yards | 1999
   22-for-47, 3 TDs | 38–28 (Texas)

2. **Colt McCoy** | 324 yards | 2007
   19-for-26, 2 TDs | 28–21 (OU)

3. **Major Applewhite** | 293 yards | 1998
   14-for-27, 2 TDs | 34–3 (Texas)

4. **Colt McCoy** | 277 yards | 2008
   28-for-35, TD | 45–35 (Texas)

5. **Peter Gardere** | 274 yards | 1992
   18-for-32, 2 TDs | 34–24 (Texas)

TEXAS

"Brandon played to the best of his ability," Cooper said, "but losing a guy on either side of the ball with that much responsibility is tough to overcome." The Sooners couldn't overcome it. On four consecutive possessions, Texas scored on drives of 89, 42, 74, and 80 yards. The first dagger came on McCoy's pass to Shipley, who settled in behind on Crow on a crossing route. Shipley scooted 37 yards to the OU 1, setting up a touchdown to put the Longhorns up 38–35. The second dagger came on UT's next drive. Out of the shotgun, McCoy handed off to Ogbonnaya on a sweep to the right. A pair of pulling linemen obliterated OU's front line of defense. Crow, who got hung up in pursuit, was a step late, and Ogbonnaya raced 62 yards to the OU 2. Two plays later, Cody Johnson punched the ball over the goal line to seal a stunning 45–35 victory for the Longhorns. "It was tough to watch," said Reynolds, who left his helmet on while watching the rest of the game sitting on the sideline. "Not being able to do anything about it, it was disheartening."

1967

TEXAS	0	0	3	6	**9**
OKLAHOMA	7	0	0	0	**7**

In 1967 there was tremendous optimism surrounding the Oklahoma program after Jim Mackenzie's first season. The Sooners had ended an eight-game losing streak to Texas and knocked off fourth-ranked Nebraska in Norman. OU also featured a plethora of rising talents like quarterback Bob Warmack, wide receiver Eddie Hinton, and center Ken Mendenhall, all native Oklahomans. Mackenzie had been named the Big 8 Coach of the Year and had the Sooners on the path back to national

prominence. OU would get there in '67. But, tragically, Mackenzie wasn't around to see it.

Though only 37, Mackenzie began having heart trouble in the off-season. Before spring practice, he suffered a slight heart flare-up that he began taking medicine for. His gradual weight gain and smoking addiction weren't helping, either. Mackenzie went through several packs of Camels a day, including five on the day of OU's win over Texas the year before.

On April 27, Mackenzie flew to Amarillo to meet with blue-chip quarterback Monte Johnson, who would eventually sign with Texas, but later transfered to OU and became a starting safety. On his way out of the office, Mackenzie stopped to chat with assistant Barry Switzer. "Barry, I'm going to get us a quarterback," he said. "Promise me one thing. You won't run anybody off today." It was the last conversation Mackenzie and Switzer ever had.

Mackenzie returned to Norman on a private plane at about 9:10 PM. "Don't shut down the engines," he told pilot Paul Finefrock. "I'll just hop out." Mackenzie appeared to be fine. But that night, he phoned the Oklahoma City heart specialist he had been seeing and complained of chest discomfort. The doctor gave Mackenzie permission to increase his meds. But shortly after his conversation with the doctor, Mackenzie suffered a massive heart attack. His wife, Sue, immediately called longtime Norman physician Mike Willard to come over and sent her daughter to get OU receivers coach Galen Hall, who lived across the street, to begin artificial respiration. Recognizing the seriousness of Mackenzie's condition, Willard called for an ambulance. Mackenzie died en route to Norman

Regional Hospital. A few of the players learned of their coach's death during a newscast that night, but most found out the next morning when they woke for classes. "Nobody could believe it. We were all numb," Mendenhall said. Warmack recalled that Mackenzie's death placed the entire team in a state of shock. "It was just devastating," he said.

Mackenzie was coach of the Sooners for 476 days. But in that short time he made a profound and lasting impact on the program and its players. "I have a lot of thoughts about Jim," Switzer said. "He was my mentor, and he didn't get to live and enjoy the great run we had at Oklahoma. We probably would have done even better had he survived."

Four days after Mackenzie's funeral, outgoing OU president George Cross promoted assistant Chuck Fairbanks to interim head coach—against the wishes of many boosters who wanted the Sooners to conduct a national search. The regents approved Fairbanks, but attached an "interim" tag to the hire. Fairbanks summarily promoted Switzer to be his offensive coordinator.

In the preseason, OU was picked to finish fourth in the Big 8. "Nobody knew how much talent we had really had," Mendenhall said. "I don't think coaches did, either." But the Sooners were loaded. Two-time All-America nose guard Granville Liggins anchored the defense, while the offense featured a balanced attack of Warmack and Hinton through the air, and future Heisman winner Steve Owens on the ground. The offense also had three players who would become All-Americans up front in Mendenhall, end Steve Zabel, and tackle Bob

Kalsu, who would later become the only professional football player to lose his life serving the country in the Vietnam War.

Mackenzie's sudden death had brought the Sooners even closer and made them even more focused on the '67 season. "We had to carry the tradition for Jim," Hinton said, "because he had such a profound statement about winning and being a champion."

OU opened the season by hammering Washington State and Maryland by a combined score of 56–0. Texas, ranked No. 4 in the preseason, started out 1–2, meanwhile, with losses to USC and Texas Tech. That trajectory for both teams continued through the first quarter of the Cotton Bowl. OU forced a Texas punt, then marched 78 yards in 59 seconds for a touchdown. Warmack keyed the drive with a pair of first-down completions. Tailback Ron Shotts capped it off with a two-yard scoring plunge over the left guard.

The Sooners continued to dominate the first half but would have no more points to show for it. "We ran up and down the field on them," Hinton said. "But we just couldn't get the ball in. Something would always happen." Two possessions after the opening touchdown, OU had the ball deep in Texas territory. But Warmack's pass at the goal line bounced off tight end Joe Killingsworth and into the arms of Texas linebacker Glen Halsell for the interception. Later in the second quarter, OU had the ball at the Texas 11, thanks to a couple of tough runs by Owens. But the drive stalled there, and OU faced fourth-and-1. Instead of going for it, Fairbanks called for the field goal.

The year before, OU had won the game behind the leg of Mike Vachon, who produced the greatest field-goal-kicking effort in school history. Vachon nailed four field goals, including a school record 43-yarder and game-clinching 41-yarder late in the fourth quarter. But never before—and not since—did a player go from OU-Texas hero to OU-Texas goat so precipitously as Vachon.

Vachon entered the '67 Texas game struggling, having missed all five of his field-goal attempts. Those struggles would continue and cost the Sooners dearly. Vachon's first attempt from 27 yards missed so badly to the right that it only made it to the 3-yard line.

OU got one final chance to score before the half, thanks to Hinton's 33-yard punt return. But Warmack's pass attempt to Killingsworth was intercepted again in the end zone. All told, the Sooners had the ball in the red zone four times in the first half—and came away with just seven points. "We should have been up at least 21–0," Warmack said.

Darrell Royal knew his team was lucky to be down one score. But he knew if his team didn't start playing better, eventually that luck would run out. "There's a hell of a fight going on out there," Royal told his players at halftime. "Why don't you get in on it?" The Longhorns came out fighting in the second half. After another squandered scoring opportunity by the Sooners, this time a Warmack fumble at the Longhorns 29, Texas finally got something going. Quarterback "Super Bill" Bradley, who had missed the '66 game with an injury, led Texas down the field, and Rob Layne—son of Texas quarterback Bobby Layne, who beat the Sooners four times in the 1940s—put UT on the board with a 35-yard field goal.

After OU was forced to punt, Bradley again had the Horns on the move. On third-and-2 from the Texas 25, he broke two tackles off the left side before being dragged down by Liggins 15 yards downfield. Bradley finished the drive with a seven-yard touchdown scamper around the left end. Layne missed the extra point. Yet despite its disastrous start, Texas led 9–7 in the fourth quarter.

The Sooners would have one final chance to win the game. After Layne missed a field goal, Owens burst through a huge hole and rumbled 49 yards to the Texas 29. After six more runs, OU had the ball again at the UT 11, facing fourth-and-short. Again, Fairbanks called for the field goal. And again, Vachon missed badly, this time to the left. Texas would hold on for the 9–7 win.

During their postgame show, OU radio color analyst Jack Ogle defended Vachon on the air, pointing out that Vachon had won the game for the Sooners the year before. When the radio crew signed off, Ogle took his earphones off, slammed them on the table, turned to play-by-play announcer Bob Barry and grunted, "They oughta kick the sonofabitch off the team."

The '67 game proved to be one of the most gut-wrenching losses to Texas in OU history. "That '67 team would have won the national championship if we had beaten Texas," Warmack said. "Just a devastating loss." The Sooners ran the table the rest of the way, including a 23–0 victory over ninth-ranked Colorado. OU climbed to fifth in the polls, then beat second-ranked Tennessee in the Orange Bowl. But in the 1960s national championships were still awarded before the bowls.

And USC was crowned national champ before escaping unranked Indiana in the Rose Bowl.

"The '67 season was special," Zabel said. "But it would have been really special to win a national championship. People in Oklahoma don't remember Big 8 champions. They only remember national champions."

1976

TEXAS	0	3	0	3	6
OKLAHOMA	0	0	0	6	6

For several years, Texas coach Darrell Royal had been suspicious that Oklahoma had been spying on his practices. Those suspicious arose in 1972 after the Sooners yelled, "Quick-kick!" as the Longhorns broke their huddle and then blocked the quick-kick for a touchdown. Turned out, OU had spied on Texas that week and knew the quick-kick was coming. Royal, however, never had any proof—until the fall of 1976.

Tony Herry, a Texas booster, was having drinks one night in Houston in December of '75 with the so-called Sooners spy, oil businessman Lonnie Williams, who formerly coached with OU defensive coordinator Larry Lacewell at Wichita State. According to Herry's account, Williams boasted after a few cocktails that he had pretended to be a painter working on UT's stadium in '72 and witnessed the Longhorns working on the quick-kick. Herry relayed the information to Texas assistant David McWilliams, who passed it along to Royal, who called Herry to get the name of this alleged spy.

Royal believed he finally had his proof. The day before the OU game, he challenged Barry Switzer and Williams to take lie-detector tests and offered to donate $10,000 to their favorite charities if they passed. Switzer declined and countered, "It's worth more money to me to have him continue to look for ghosts." Switzer's response further exasperated Royal, who blurted to AP reporter Robert Heard, "Why, those sorry bastards, I don't trust 'em on anything." The quote made its way into print.

Without warning, the rivalry suddenly had reached unprecedented levels of tense bitterness. During pregame warmups, Switzer and Royal avoided each other. Switzer avoided midfield, while Royal stood on his side of the 47 smacking gum with his back turned to the south end zone. OU fans chanted, "Sorry bastards!" Texas fans uncharacteristically even showed up early for this one to get their boos in.

Adding to the awkwardness, President Gerald Ford attended the game and would walk Royal and Switzer out to the field before flipping the coin. Not even the leader of the free world could diffuse this Red River standoff. "Darrell accuses of spying, and it's the most embarrassing moment, but at the same it was kind of hilarious considering the circumstances," recalled Switzer, who after retiring admitted in his book that OU had spied in '72. "Well, President Ford shook hands with Darrell, then he turns around and shakes hands with me. Darrell and I, neither one of us acted like the other was there. The papers had been having a field day with us. So I don't say a damn thing to Darrell, and he doesn't say anything to me. We walk down there, and Ford had to be thinking, *What the hell? These guys*

are really serious, they don't even speak to each other. Ford is trying to make small talk, and we're not having anything to do with it. We walk down to right under the goal post. Well, some redneck from Oklahoma over to my right hollers at the top of his lungs. He had one of those voices you could hear for a hundred yards. Must have called hogs his whole life or something. Because he stands up and yells at the top of his lungs, 'Who are those two assholes with Switzer?!' Of course, the south end of the stadium erupts in laughter, everybody starts dying laughing. Of course, I felt like this high, so embarrassed. I'm thinking, *Sonofabitch, I can't believe that guy said that.*"

The game proved to be far less exciting than the buildup. Without starting quarterback Dean Blevins, who had been hospitalized that week, OU fell back into a vanilla game plan and went scoreless through three quarters. Texas clung to a 6–0 lead on a pair of Russell Erxleben field goals and was simply trying to run out the clock. Instead, with just over five minutes to play, OU tackle David Hudgens belted Texas running back Ivey Suber to jar the ball loose, and Zac Henderson pounced on it to give the Sooners possession at the Texas 37. After being outplayed the entire game, OU had a chance to win. The Sooners opened up the playbook and started calling the option. "We started doing what we do best," said quarterback Thomas Lott. Lott kept for eight yards—OU's longest rushing play the entire game—to get the drive going, and Horace Ivory finished it off with a one-yard prance left into the end zone. The Sooners were an extra point away from winning their sixth in a row in the series. An extra point Uwe von Schamann would never get to attempt. Center Kevin Craig snapped high to holder Bud Hebert, who couldn't bring the ball down. A game both sides

wanted more than ever ended in a 6–6 tie. "They say a tie is better than a loss," Henderson said. "I don't know about that. That was one of the worst feelings in the world. It was a nothing feeling."

Royal was just as sick. Before he got to the dressing room, he bent over and dry-heaved. He then opened his press conference by apologizing for the "sorry bastards" quote.

The Longhorns finished 5–5–1, their worst season with Royal as coach. After the season, Royal retired and would say of the '76 OU game, "I never felt as sick about a game as I did that one. I wanted that game more than any I competed in or coached in." Royal was summarily inducted into the Texas Sports Hall of Fame. Sixteen years later, the Hollis, Oklahoma, native and OU grad was inducted into the Oklahoma Sports Hall of Fame, as well.

1958

TEXAS	0	8	0	7	**15**
OKLAHOMA	0	0	6	8	**14**

Before the 1957 season, Texas called on a Sooner to resurrect its floundering football program. Born and raised in Hollis, Oklahoma, Darrell Royal arrived in Norman in 1946, the same year as Bud Wilkinson. With Royal's help as an All-America quarterback, Wilkinson welded the Sooners into a powerhouse that would dominate college football for the next decade.

Following in the footsteps of his mentor, Royal opted to pursue a career in coaching and landed an assistant's job at North

TEXAS

STREAKS OU FANS HATE: 1958–1970

TEXAS GOES 12–1

In the 1950s OU won an NCAA record 47 straight games and brought home three national championships. That level of excellence is impossible for Bud Wilkinson to maintain. And in the 1960s the Sooners come back to earth while Texas ascends under OU football great Darrell Royal, hired by the Longhorns in 1957.

The following year, Royal inserts backup quarterback Bobby Lackey on third down from the OU 7-yard line, and Lackey tosses a touchdown to Bob Bryant with 3:10 left in the game to pull off the 15–14 win. But 1963 proves to be the defining matchup, and Wilkinson's final OU-Texas game. For the first time, the two teams enter ranked No. 1 and No. 2. But Tommy Nobis and Scott Appleton shut down the Sooners offense and spearhead the Longhorns to a convincing 28–7 victory, giving Royal his sixth straight win over Wilkinson.

The Longhorns go on to win their first national title, and after the season Wilkinson retires.

Carolina. Royal quickly ascended up the coaching ladder and earned head jobs at Mississippi State and Washington. Royal was only 32 years old, but athletics director Dana X. Bible couldn't find a coach anywhere who didn't rave about Royal—Wilkinson more than anyone. "Dad was instrumental in getting Darrell the job," said Jay Wilkinson, Bud's youngest son. "They had a very deep friendship."

Royal took a risk in taking the Texas job. His predecessors, Blair Cherry and Ed Price, had been forced out because they couldn't top Wilkinson, who had a five-game winning streak running against the Horns. "Texas had to develop a football

tradition," Royal would say. "It had it once, but lost it. When we get one, maybe we can stop that bloodletting up at Dallas and turn it into a good show."

In Royal's first season, the Longhorns showed marked improvement after finishing 1–9 the year before. Texas beat Georgia, Arkansas, and played the mighty Sooners so valiantly in a 21–7 loss the Austin media hailed the performance. "That was about as tough a game as I remember," OU halfback Jakie Sandefer recalled. "They hit like hell."

After the season, a crucial meeting of the NCAA rules committee changed college football. It would change the 1958 Red River Rivalry, too. Spearheaded by Michigan athletics director Fritz Crisler, the committee voted to allow teams to go for two points after touchdowns. The impetus was to reduce the number of ties in the game. Wilkinson, who was also on the committee, was a big proponent of the rule change and voted for the two-point conversion. Royal publicly opposed the change—but he would become the first coach to win a game because of it.

OU's unprecedented 47-game winning streak had finally ended the year before, but the Sooners still opened the '58 season ranked second in the country and were unbeaten going into the game against Texas. The Longhorns entered the Cotton Bowl undefeated, as well, after three narrow victories, but were still two-touchdown underdogs. After all, Texas hadn't defeated the Sooners in seven years. "The only way anybody's going to beat Oklahoma is go out there and whip 'em jaw to jaw; any team that played Oklahoma timidly would be humiliated," Royal said the week leading up to the game. "They get a yellow dog running downhill and they'll strap him real good."

Royal knew, though, it would take more than a bold spirit to take down the Sooners. In the second quarter, on fourth-and-4 from the OU 10, Royal gambled and went for the first down. Quarterback Rene Ramirez rolled left and hit George Blanch for a touchdown. Then Royal gambled again. "We decided before the game that, if we scored first, we'd go for two points on a play so plain vanilla it would catch them by surprise," Royal would say. "When we lined up for two they had to be expecting some fluzzie-duzzie play." Instead Texas handed the ball to Don Allen off left guard. With H.G. Anderson the lead blocker, Allen crashed over Sandefer for the two-point conversion, giving the Longhorns an 8–0 lead "I hit him right in the hole, but he wouldn't go down," Sandefer said. "I still have a knot in my shoulder from that play. It hurt me the whole damn year."

The two-point conversion changed the complexion of the game. In the third quarter OU finally got on the board on a Dick Carpenter touchdown run. Bobby Boyd's pass for the two-point conversion, however, fell incomplete. But in the fourth quarter, the Sooners converted off a wacky turnover. After the Longhorns fumbled a handoff, the ball ended up on the back of running back Mike Dowdle. OU's Jim Davis picked up the ball and rumbled 24 yards for a touchdown. Boyd converted the two-point pass this time, and the Sooners led 14–8, seemingly headed for their seventh consecutive Red River victory.

Texas, which had not registered a first down the entire second half, took over on its own 26 with 6:50 left. Trying to get anything going, Royal inserted backup Vince Matthews at quarterback. At first, the substitution appeared to be a disaster—the Longhorns faced third-and-18. But Matthews flipped a screen to Blanch for 11 yards, then found Bobby

Bryant in the flat for the first down. Five plays later, the Longhorns had third-and-goal at the Sooners 7.

Royal sent the taller Bobby Lackey back in at quarterback for Matthews, and Lackey responded by finding Bryant over the middle for a touchdown with a jump pass. Lackey kicked the extra point, then intercepted the Sooners on the ensuing possession to seal the stunning 15–14 victory. "Desire did it for us," Royal said afterward. "They had speed, aggressiveness—in fact just about everything. But enough fire-up can offset all of that. It did this afternoon."

After the game, OU president George Cross went to the Texas dressing room to congratulate Royal on the landmark victory. The room was filled with players, assistant coaches, even fans. But Royal was nowhere to be found. An assistant told Cross that Royal had gone behind the building. "Following this lead, I went outside and found Royal leaning against the back of the building," Cross later wrote. "His face was colorless, except for a sort of greenish-blue tint around his mouth. He was obviously ill; it was apparent that he had lost at least part of his lunch." When asked what was wrong, Royal replied, "It just didn't seem right to beat Mr. Wilkinson."

1977

TEXAS	0	10	0	3	**13**
OKLAHOMA	3	0	3	0	**6**

In 1977 Texas finally beat the Sooners with the best player Barry Switzer ever saw and a backup quarterback nobody ever heard of.

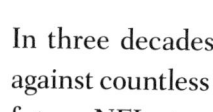

In three decades coaching college football, Switzer faced off against countless Heisman Trophy winners, All-Americans, and future NFL stars. None better, however, than Earl Campbell. "John Elway and Barry Sanders, they were great players," Switzer said. "But Earl Campbell was the greatest player I ever saw."

Switzer won many head-to-head recruiting battles against the Longhorns. But the one for Campbell he would lose. Texas coach Darrell Royal dispatched assistant Ken Dabbs to the Tyler, Texas, Ramada Inn for 17 straight days to recruit Campbell, who signed with the Longhorns.

Before 1974, college football had never seen a running back like Campbell, whom Switzer believes could have played in the NFL right out of Tyler Lee High School. "When you saw guys hit him, it was like BBs bouncing off a Sherman tank," said OU halfback Joe Washington. Hard-hitting Sooners safety Scott Hill recalled such a run-in with Campbell. "I remember Lee Roy and Dewey [Selmon] had Earl, and he was dragging them forward with his back to me," Hill said. "I had a 10-yard running start and hit him straight in the back. I thought I was going to bust him good. Instead I bounced right off him."

Yet even with Campbell carrying the load offensively, Texas failed to beat the program Campbell spurned his first three years. End Jimbo Elrod jarred the ball out of Campbell's arms in '74, leading to OU's game-winning field goal. In '75 and '76 the Sooners also limited Campbell to less than 100 yards rushing in a 24–17 OU win and 6–6 tie, after which Sooners defensive coordinator Larry Lacewell proclaimed, "They've had Campbell three years now, and he hasn't dominated a game yet."

STREAKS OU FANS HATE: 1977–1984

TEXAS GOES 5–2–1

The Sooners win national titles between 1975 and 1985, but sandwiched between is another series of struggles in the Cotton Bowl. And the bookends of this streak are the toughest to take.

In 1977 place-kicker Russell Erxleben booms 64- and 58-yard field goals to put Texas up 13–6. In the final minutes, quarterback Thomas Lott orchestrates a potential game-tying drive. But on fourth-and-1 from the Texas 6-yard line, Lott is stuffed, and the Horns go on to win.

OU fans remember 1984 as even more painful. Keith Stanberry intercepts Todd Dodge's pass in the end zone, but official Butch Clark rules Stanberry out of bounds, allowing Texas to kick a last-play field goal for the 15–15 tie.

T E X A S

But in 1977 Campbell showed up to camp 25 pounds lighter than the 245 he had played at the previous three years. Not only did it help him remain healthy, Campbell's speed improved. Royal, meanwhile, had retired in the off-season and was replaced by Fred Akers, who scrapped the wishbone and installed the I formation offense to feature Campbell more effectively. "When he got seven yards of steam going, he was hard to stop," said OU safety Zac Henderson. "I wish they would have waited until I graduated before putting Earl in the I."

For the second time in three years, OU and Texas entered their game each ranked in the top five. The Sooners, however, were coming off their biggest noncoference regular season win in school history—a 29–28 victory at Ohio State on a last-second Uwe von Schamann field goal. Few were picking the Longhorns to end OU's six-game unbeaten streak in

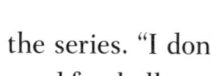

the series. "I don't know if anybody believes it, but we have a good football team," Campbell said the week of the game. "We know OU has a great team, but I think we are ready."

To Campbell's horror, the game got off to an awful start for the Horns. Starting quarterback Mark McBath turned an ankle in the first quarter and had to be helped off the field. Not long after that, backup Joe Aune took a hit to his knee while handing off to Campbell and had to leave the game, too. With still 2:13 remaining in the first quarter, the Longhorns were down to their third-string quarterback.

Randy McEachern was not exactly destined for Red River greatness. He stood just 5'11", weighed only 170 pounds, and was so buried on the depth chart he didn't even get mentioned in the Texas media guide. Against OU the year before, McEachern worked in the press box as a spotter for the Exxon radio network after undergoing knee surgery. McEachern's parents were so sure their son wouldn't get to play this time, either, they didn't even bother driving up from Houston for the game. Instead they listened to it on the radio.

As McEachern came in for Aune with his hands shaking, Texas tackle Rick Ingraham grabbed McEachern's jersey, pulled him face mask–to–face mask, and growled, "You give the fuckin' ball to Earl and get the hell out of the way." Unfortunately for the Sooners, McEachern would do more than that. With game knotted at 3–3 late in the second quarter, McEachern completed passes of 23 and 18 yards to Alfred Jackson to drive the Horns into OU territory. Campbell took over from there.

Cutting off a block from Oklahoma native Steve Hall, Campbell broke through the OU front 24 yards for a touchdown with just over a minute to go before half. "That drive killed us," Switzer would say.

Place-kicker Russell Erxleben and the Texas defense did the rest. Erxleben, who had converted an OU-Texas record 64-yard field goal in the first half, nailed a 58-yarder in the fourth quarter to put the Longhorns up by a touchdown. Then Brad Shearer and Johnnie Johnson stuffed OU quarterback Thomas Lott on fourth down inside the Texas 5-yard line to hand Switzer his first Red River loss, 13–6.

Campbell, who would go on to become Texas' first Heisman Trophy winner, ran for 124 yards on 23 carries—his first and only 100-yard game in the series. McEachern finished with only four completions, but two of those spearheaded the only touchdown drive of the game. "McEachern showed a lot of courage and poise, coming in for the first time ever in a big game and doing a great job running the team," Akers told reporters outside the Longhorns locker room. "He made some decisions on the field that were tough, but they were right."

The Longhorns went on to an undefeated regular season, but lost to Notre Dame in the Cotton Bowl to fall short of the national championship. After graduating the following year, McEachern married a Texas cheerleader and the couple settled in Austin. Ironically, their son, Hays, would end up in Norman holding kicks for the Sooners his final two seasons of college.

1962

TEXAS	0	9	0	0	**9**
OKLAHOMA	0	6	0	0	**6**

Armed with a pair of fifth-stringers, including one who hitch-hiked his way to the Cotton Bowl drunk in the back of a farm truck, the Sooners nearly knocked off No. 1–ranked Texas in 1962.

Few OU football players were as hated as much as Lance Rentzel was upon his arrival to Norman. On a team full of farm boys and petroleum roughnecks, Rentzel was a private-school kid from the city. Starring for Oklahoma City Casady, Rentzel was a high school All-American, and the players who didn't know before, found out while Rentzel was moving in. Committing social suicide of the highest order, Rentzel allowed his mother to put his high school trophies and plaques in his dorm room. That didn't sit well with Rentzel's older teammates. "That really did it," said Rentzel, who permanently earned the nickname "Tommy Trophy." "Everyone on the team would run across the field to hit me. They just beat the shit out of me."

As a result, Rentzel grew to hate football. Even though he had been one of Bud Wilkinson's top recruits in the Class of '61, Rentzel remained on the scout team as a sophomore. After one notably grueling two-a-day, Rentzel decided he'd had enough. "I said, 'That's it, I'm quitting,'" he said. "'I'll just be in a frat or something.'" Rentzel went home to break the news to his mom. But she convinced him to at least wait until his father got back from business in South America before quitting. So Rentzel begrudgingly went back to practice. Adding injury to insult,

Rentzel broke his thumb in practice the next day. "I figured I might as well wait until my thumb heals before I quit," he said.

A couple of weeks later, Rentzel finally got his hand out of the cast and had every intention of quitting that week, as the rest of his teammates prepared to play Texas. "After practice, I was going to go to Wilkinson and tell him that football wasn't for me," Rentzel said. As he was waiting for the opportune time, Rentzel was playing catch with fifth-string quarterback Joe Fletcher, who came to OU without a scholarship and had to sell hot dogs during home games his freshman year for money. Rentzel wasn't even suited up and was wearing jeans and loafers. It's unclear what Wilkinson saw that day that made him even notice these two fifth-stringers playing catch to the side. But Wilkinson saw something.

Wilkinson called both boys over and essentially drew up a trick play in the dirt he had just thought up. He placed Fletcher—who had already moved to halfback because he cut his tongue the week before and could barely speak—in the backfield, and Rentzel at flanker. Wilkinson ordered the quarterback to pitch the ball to Fletcher, and Fletcher to throw a halfback pass downfield to Rentzel. "I run downfield, I can't get any traction, I'm slipping everywhere," Rentzel. "The play was awful. I have no idea why, but Wilkinson brings us over and says, 'That looks good.'"

Wilkinson didn't have any more spots left on the team plane. But he told Rentzel if he could get down to Dallas on his own, he would suit up for the game. "I was planning on taking the homecoming queen with me down there," Rentzel said. "I figured, *Hey, maybe she'll like me more if I'm suiting up for the*

game." So the next day Rentzel loaded his 1957 powder-blue Thunderbird with a case of beer in the backset and headed south. But the joy ride Rentzel had planned quickly turned into a fiasco.

A few miles outside of Marietta, the Thunderbird started leaking oil and broke down. Rentzel and his date were stuck in the middle of nowhere. "We waited and waited," he said. "Finally, this guy, a farmer, picks us up. He only had room for one in the front, so I got in the back." Also in the back were a couple of pigs and a couple of chickens. Rentzel decided it was time to get really drunk. "This girl had to be looking at me like, *Why am I with this idiot?"* he said. "I'm thinking, *How humiliating is my life going to be? I was an All-American two years ago. Look at me now."* By the time the truck crossed the Red River, Rentzel had finished his first six-pack. Before the truck got to Dallas, he had polished off two more.

The truck, however, wasn't going to Fort Worth, where the team was staying, so the two had to hail a cab from Dallas. By the time they got to the team hotel, Rentzel's hotel room had been given away. So the two took another cab and started driving west until they found a motel with a vacancy on OU-Texas weekend. "I don't even know what time I'm supposed to be at the stadium the next day," Rentzel said. Nervous he would oversleep and miss the game, Rentzel stayed up all night. "I don't even know what time the game is supposed to start," he said. "All I know is that it's at the Cotton Bowl." Out of money from the night before, Rentzel borrowed money from his date and took a cab to the stadium before 8:00. Kickoff would not be for another six hours. "Just one humiliation after another," Rentzel said. The humiliations were far from done.

Texas coach Darrell Royal (kneeling) looks over the Cotton Bowl field during the Longhorns' 9–6 victory over the Sooners on October 15, 1962.

Rentzel, who arrived at the Texas State Fair two hours before the team would, had no idea where he was supposed to be or how he was going to get inside the stadium. Still reeking of beer and farm animals from the night before, Rentzel tried telling his story to the security guards, who thought he was a deranged alcoholic. When the guards couldn't find Rentzel anywhere in the game program, they threatened to have him arrested if he didn't leave.

Unsure of what to do, Rentzel scarfed down a couple of hot dogs at the fair, rode the ferris wheel, then just started walking

around the stadium, over and over. Finally he ran into OU trainer Ken Rawlinson, who wasn't aware Rentzel was supposed to suit up that day. "He says, 'Rentzel, have you been drinking?' I say, 'Yes, but you don't understand. There were these pigs and chickens and my car broke down and I was depressed and I'm supposed to suit up,'" Rentzel recalled. "He says, 'Rentzel, you're an embarrassment,' then reluctantly lets me in the locker room."

Instead of dressing with the team, Rentzel suited up in tiny stall outside the locker room. "About noon, there's a guy knocking on the dressing room door, saying he was a football player," Fletcher said. "Someone opens the door, and there's Rentzel, all suited up."

On the field, the OU defense gave the Longhorns everything they wanted, forcing Texas to punt four times in the first quarter. Only after the Longhorns were mistakenly allowed a fifth down in the second quarter, did they finally get on the board with a 26-yard field goal.

Problem was, OU couldn't move the ball, either. And after UT's Perry McWilliams recovered a fumbled pitch in the end zone, the Longhorns led 9–0 with only a couple of minutes before halftime.

After another negative rushing play, Wilkinson grew desperate and—to their surprise—called over Fletcher and Rentzel, who was still severely hungover, and sent them in with their play, "58 Special." "I couldn't believe this was happening," Rentzel said. "If I thought I was actually going to play, I wouldn't have gotten so drunk the night before."

Like they had practiced for all of two minutes, Fletcher lined up at left halfback, and Rentzel flexed out to the right. Fletcher got the pitch, ran right, and looked downfield for Rentzel, who was well-covered. "I ran 30 yards or so and figured I'd better turn," Rentzel said. "As I turn, I think, *No way is this going to work*. But right then, the ball hits me in the chest. A perfectly executed fluke," which also resulted in a 39-yard gain, the longest play of the game.

Ecstatic they hadn't screwed up, Fletcher and Rentzel were jogging to the sideline when Wilkinson waved them back to run the play to the other side. This time, Rentzel blew by future New York Jets cornerback Jim Hudson, and off the pitch, Fletcher lofted a perfect pass to Rentzel at the goal line for a 34-yard touchdown. "The whole thing was pure luck," said Rentzel, who just held the ball up to the OU fans until the official came and took it from him. "No skill involved. Just absolute pure luck."

Despite the huge momentum boost going into the half, OU did little offensively the rest of the way and fell 9–7. In fact, outside of Rentzel's two catches, the Sooners gained just 94 yards all game. In the final seconds, fisticuffs broke out between Longhorns running back Tommy Lucas and OU end Rick McCurdy, after McCurdy threw dirt into the face of a Texas player. The benches cleared, and players wildly threw punches at one another, including Rentzel, who accidentally smacked one of his own teammates.

Even though it was a loss, the game proved to be a turning point for Rentzel and the Sooners. In what Wilkinson believed

would be a rebuilding year, OU won win its final seven regular season games, captured the Big 8 title, and earned a trip to the Orange Bowl. Rentzel, who almost quit football, went on to a prolific receiving career with the Dallas Cowboys.

1989

TEXAS	15	6	0	7	28
OKLAHOMA	7	0	7	10	24

On February 27, 1989, Oklahoma football was changed forever. Quarterback Charles Thompson appeared on the cover of *Sports Illustrated* in an orange jumpsuit, sending the program in a tailspin. By June, Barry Switzer, the fourth-winningest coach in college football history, had resigned and OU was slapped with NCAA sanctions. Gary Gibbs, a defensive assistant under Switzer for 14 years, was tapped to be his successor and clean up the program.

Yet for all its turmoil, OU was an 18-point favorite to beat Texas a fifth straight time in '89. The Longhorns were coming off a 4–7 season and had already lost twice. Having nothing to lose, David McWilliams turned his offense over to a freshman quarterback by the name of Peter Gardere. This seemingly innocuous lineup shuffle would have devastating consequences for the Sooners over the next four years.

After falling behind early, OU roared back from a 21–7 halftime deficit to retake the lead. Quarterback Tink Collins teamed with Arthur Guess on a 41-yard touchdown pass play to bring the Sooners to within 21–14. A 30-yard field goal by R.D. Lashar

STREAKS OU FANS HATE: 1989–1999

TEXAS GOES 8–2–1

The 1990s is a decade to forget. Texas supremacy is one reason why. In 1991 OU waltzes in ranked sixth while Texas staggers in after a 1–2 start. But, after a quick score, a Sooners offense averaging 38 points a game is completely handcuffed. The Texas offense does little more. But the game is decided when Bubba Jacques scoops up a fumble and races 20 yards for Texas' only touchdown. The Longhorns hold on, 10–7. Gary Gibbs, who goes 1–5 against Texas, is ultimately fired, and Sooners football falls into a tailspin until Bob Stoops is hired in 1999.

T E X A S

narrowed the margin to 21–17. Then running back Ike Lewis, who replaced injured starter Mike Gaddis, scored on a one-yard run with 3:42 to go to give OU the 24–21 lead.

Coming into the game, Texas hadn't beaten the Sooners since 1983 and had barely beaten lowly Rice the week before on a fourth-quarter, game-winning touchdown drive engineered by Gardere. But in this game, Gardere had done nothing in the second half to suggest he was capable of doing the same to the Sooners.

Starting at the UT 34, Gardere found Tony Jones for eight yards, then Johnny Walker for 17. Jones picked up eight more on another reception. All of a sudden, the Longhorns were moving, and quickly. "We really felt good when we went out there," Gardere would say. "We knew what we had to do, and everyone thought we were going to do it."

The Sooners appeared to seal the win with a 10-yard sack of Gardere. But defensive end Corey Mayfield was called for roughing the passer, giving Texas a first down at the OU 25 instead of second-and-20 at the 40. "That certainly changed the momentum," Gibbs said. But on second-and-10, Gibbs brought the blitz again. This time Gardere was ready for it. Stepping up into the pocket, Gardere found Walker isolated in single coverage on a post route. He lofted the ball to the goal line, and Walker hauled it in. Texas 28, OU 24. "It was mine," Walker said after the game. "If he just got it in my general direction, I was going to get it."

The Sooners still had 1:33 to try and make something happen, but Collins was sacked on the final play to end the game. "Peter said in the huddle, 'We've got to do it,'" Walker said. "'We've got to have the touchdown. Let's get it done.'" Gardere would get it done against the Sooners again, and again, and again. And would finish his career as the only quarterback on either side to go 4–0 in the series as a starter.

2005

TEXAS	14	10	7	14	**45**
OKLAHOMA	6	0	0	6	**12**

Going into the 2005 Red River Shootout, the Sooners had outscored the Longhorns 189–54 over their last five meetings—all convincing Oklahoma wins. Never before in the history of the rivalry had one side so clobbered the other. But for the first time since Bob Stoops and Mack Brown began squaring off from opposite sidelines, Brown had the quarterback advantage. A Superman-sized one. And that would make all the difference.

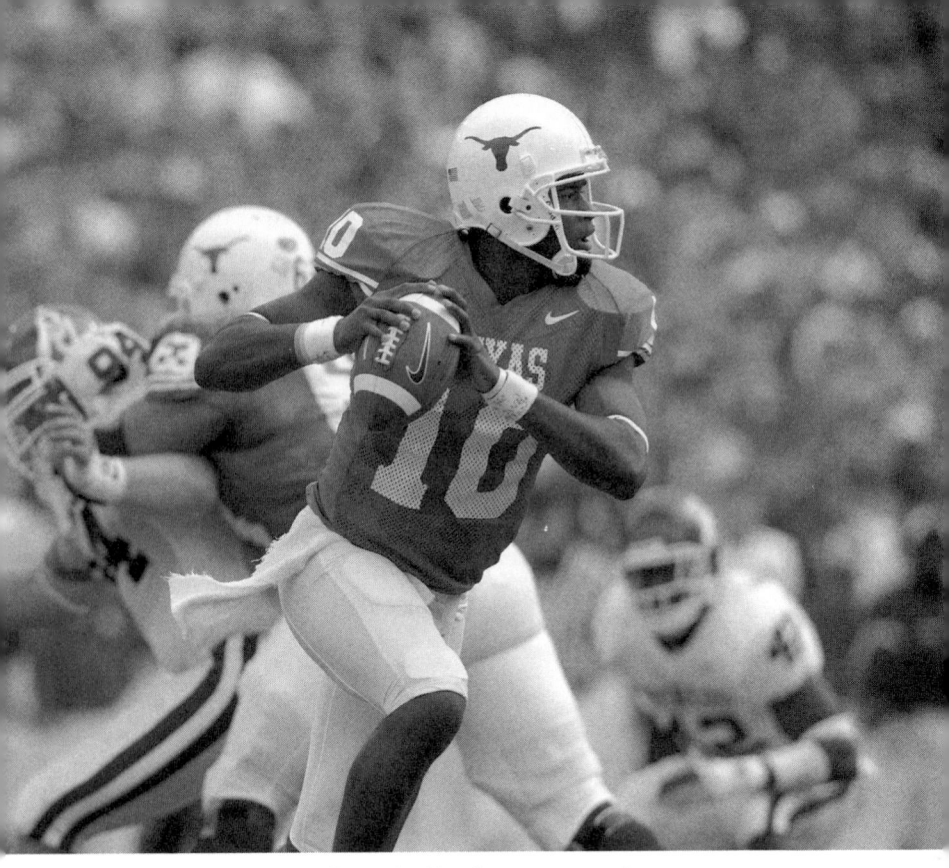

Longhorns QB Vince Young rolls out, looking for an open receiver or an opportunity to take off, in Texas' 45–12 rout of Oklahoma in 2005.

The Sooners entered the '05 season coming off back-to-back national championship appearances. The return of 2004 Red River hero and Heisman runner-up, tailback Adrian Peterson, gave Stoops hope his team could make a run at a third. But this would prove to be far from a national championship–caliber club. Gone were quarterback Jason White, wideout Mark Clayton, and offensive tackle Jammal Brown, three of the best players to ever don the crimson jerseys. The Sooners were young and inexperienced on the offensive and defensive lines, wide receiver, and defensive back, but most especially at quarterback, where redshirt freshman Rhett Bomar was taking over.

It took one game for Sooner Nation to realize this would be a rebuilding a year. OU was stunned in the opener at home by TCU. In that game, Bomar and Paul Thompson combined to complete just 13 of 31 passes. Then two weeks later in their road game, the Sooners were hammered at UCLA by 17. OU entered the Cotton Bowl a battered team. Yet there was a sense of invincibility surrounding the Sooners when it came to playing Texas. "We really thought we were going to beat Texas," recalled fullback J.D. Runnels. "We thought we were just as good." As it would play out, the Sooners were not. Nowhere close, in fact. And Vince Young would be the only invincible one out on the field.

Young had shown signs against OU the previous two years he might emerge into an elite quarterback. Even though the Sooners had obliterated Texas 65–13 in '03, Young rushed for 127 yards and threw for 135 more as a freshman. "Shutting down Vince was key," said OU linebacker Rufus Alexander. "We thought if we could do that, we'd have a chance

STREAKS OU FANS HATE: 2005–2009

TEXAS GOES 4–1

After being berated by his own fan base for getting shellacked by Bob Stoops, Mack Brown turns the table on his rival. The Longhorns dominate in 2005 and 2006, but Texas' landmark win comes in 2008, when the Sooners arrive ranked No. 1. OU jumps out to a 14–3 lead, but Jordan Shipley's kickoff return for a touchdown sparks the Texas comeback.

to win." Instead, Young ran wild. And Peterson did not. Because of a sprained ankle, Peterson was limited to three early carries for 10 yards, then handed off the offensive load to Bomar. OU would finally find out what life was like without the edge at quarterback. "We hadn't experienced that the last three years because we had J-White," said fullback J.D. Runnels.

The Sooners failed to produce a play for more than nine yards until there was 12:04 left and they were trailing 38–6. Young, meanwhile, sparkled. On the opening drive, he led the Longhorns 82 yards, completing all five of his passes, including a 15-yard touchdown to Ramonce Taylor, giving Texas its first lead against the Sooners in three years. A lead the Horns would not surrender. OU grinded out a pair of field goals, but Jamaal Charles answered with an 80-yard touchdown on the first snap of Texas' ensuing drive. From there, it was all burnt orange, the dagger coming on a 64-yard touchdown bomb from Young to Billy Pittman that gave the Horns a 24–6 lead with 17 seconds before halftime. Texas cruised to a 45–12 victory, snapping the Sooners' stranglehold in the series. "That was a big swing," Stoops would say afterward. "We're hanging in there, with a chance to make some plays, and we don't. That was tough to overcome."

Young would go on to lead Texas to the national championship, as the Longhorns knocked off USC in the Rose Bowl 41–38. "That pretty much summarized that year," Runnels said. "We played for two national titles and lose the second to USC. And Texas turns around and beats them."

2

MOMENTS WE HATE

SISCO MAKES SOONERS SICK

Through all the wars, elections, and heated sporting competitions, the record shows that only one man has been hung in effigy on the University of Oklahoma campus. His name was Sisco.

Under a first-year coach named Bud Wilkinson, OU's 1947 season opened with promise. The Sooners beat the University of Detroit on the road, then knocked off Texas A&M. But up next was third-ranked Texas, which had defeated the Sooners in seven consecutive seasons. Wilkinson's assistant, Dutch Fehring, called Texas "the greatest collegiate team ever assembled" and said that if the Sooners and Horns both played well, "they will outscore us six touchdowns to two." Fehring and his superior were prone to exaggeration. But the Longhorns—led by hard-nosed fullback Tom Landry and the country's best quarterback, Sooners killer Bobby Layne—were indeed loaded.

Early, OU hung tough. After a Layne touchdown pass, the Sooners countered with Jack Mitchell's three-yard scoring scamper to tie the game 7–7. But late in the first half, the Sooners were "Siscoed," a term in the Oklahoma lexicon that

has become synonymous with "screwed." With the game still tied, Texas had the ball at the OU 3-yard line with 20 seconds left. The Horns got to the 1, then quickly lined up for another play. "Before the game, everyone had agreed that the scoreboard clock would be the official time," said Jay Wilkinson, Bud's youngest son. On the next play, UT running back Randall Clay was stuffed for no gain as the final seconds ticked off the clock. Half over, right? Not so.

Official Jack Sisco, who had signaled "touchdown," then "timeout" after realizing Clay had not scored, declared that one of the UT players had called timeout from under the pile. Sisco said that because he had signaled "touchdown," he was unable to notify the scoreboard operator of the timeout before the clock ran out. Wilkinson was furious. He tore off his cap and rushed the field. "Dad always told us, if he hadn't been a first-year head coach, he would have just taken the team off the field," Jay Wilkinson said. "But he didn't have the confidence then to take what would have been very bold action." Instead, UT was granted another play with the scoreboard showing no time left. And a play more controversial than the one before it followed.

After Layne and halfback Jimmy Canady fumbled a handoff exchange, the ball ended up back in Layne's hands. Squatting, he wheeled around and pitched the ball to Clay, who then dashed around a pair of Sooners bemused about what had just happened. The OU players protested Layne's knee had been down before he pitched the ball. "I was right there, close by down low and right at that end," said former OU quarterback Claude Arnold, who hadn't joined the team yet, but was sitting in the stands that day. "Bobby Layne's knee was definitely down."

TEXAS

TEXAS COACHES IN THE COLLEGE FOOTBALL HALL OF FAME

Name	UT's coach	Inducted
D.X. Bible	1937–1946	1951
Darrell Royal	1957–1976	1983

Two officials thought he was down, too. But Sisco didn't see it that way and overruled them, handing the Horns a 14–7 half-time lead. As the teams ran off the field, Wilkinson charged through the UT band to confront Sisco and accidentally knocked over a piccolo player on the way.

In the second half, the controversial calls continued to flow against the Sooners. OU end Jim Tyree threw a powerful block to spring halfback Darrell Royal loose on a punt return, but officials flagged Tyree for clipping, placing the ball at the OU 1. With great field position, Texas scored on its next possession.

The Sooners valiantly tried to overcome the Sisco calls, and in the fourth quarter Mitchell's 72-yard touchdown run off a lateral from George Thomas trimmed the deficit to 21–14. But from there, all hell broke loose. On the ensuing posses-sion, Royal intercepted Layne to seemingly set the Sooners up with a chance to tie. But Sisco flagged OU guard Stanley West with roughing the passer, handing the ball back to the Horns. "West and I rushed him but I was in front and hit [Layne] just as he threw the ball," guard Buddy Burris later said. "But I hit him clean." Later on the drive, Clay appeared to have been

stopped at the line of scrimmage. But officials allowed the play to continue. Clay popped out of the scrum and circled around for a touchdown. By then, OU fans had had enough. Scores of pop bottles and seat cushions began raining down from the stands. Players on both sides dashed to midfield to avoid getting plunked. "The field was plum full of stuff OU people had thrown down there," recalled OU end Merle Dinkins. "Wasn't any doubt who they were aiming for."

After the field was cleared minutes later, Texas—boosted by the series of calls in its favor—went on to win 34–14. After the final whistle, OU fans lobbed more bottles from the stands. "They were coming right over my head," Arnold said. "I had never seen anything like that. It was scary." Royal grabbed his future wife, Edith, placed his helmet on her head, and ran with her to the tunnel to take cover. Fights broke out in the stands, and several OU fans made a run to the field to try and grab Sisco, who actually had to punch out one charging fan in self-defense. "They would have killed him, if they could have gotten to him," Dinkins said. A police car was driven to midfield to take Sisco and the other officials through the tunnel. "They were beating on the windows of that car while it left the field," said OU halfback Tommy Gray. One ill-advised fan smashed one of the cops with a bottle, knocking him off the fender of the police car. "The police rolled him so fast, you couldn't believe," Gray said. Bottled drinks would never be served at the Cotton Bowl again.

Back in Norman, close to 1,000 students gathered Sunday night to hang Sisco in effigy, singing "Don't Send My Boy to Texas" and "Boomer Sooner" as they strung the dummy to an elm in front of the administration building. "The students

were in an uproar," recalled OU end Ed Lisak. The students intended to burn the effigy, too, but someone ran off with the body. The next night, a crowd of 3,000 gathered and burned a new dummy of Sisco in a campus parking lot to the chant, "Jack Sisco's body lies a-moldering in the grave."

Years later, Sisco dared to travel to Shawnee, Oklahoma, for a business luncheon, and Dinkins was at the same event. "Everyone there wanted to see if I would knock the hell out of him," Dinkins said. "I just looked at him and said, 'It's a wonder you didn't get killed coming up this way.'"

LOTT IS STUFFED

After committing seven turnovers against Texas in 1980, Oklahoma quarterback J.C. Watts later said he wished he had "sunglasses and a Panama hat" so he could leave the Cotton Bowl without being noticed. Thomas Lott had the same feeling three years earlier. Except he was not able to escape town incognito.

The man of a hundred bandanas had no love for the Longhorns despite growing up in San Antonio. As a senior at Jay High School, Lott was a *Parade* All-America quarterback, but didn't even make all-district. The player who did, Ted Constanzo, was white and headed to Texas. Lott was black and undecided.

Lott already had bad feelings about the Longhorns when he took an official visit to Austin. There, coach Darrell Royal asked how the trip was going, and what other schools he was considering. After Lott mentioned Oklahoma, Royal flew off

the handle. "Oklahoma? How the hell are you even going to consider going to the University of Oklahoma?" Royal asked Lott. "How can you think about leaving the state of Texas after all the state of Texas has done for you?" Lott couldn't recall the state of Texas ever running sprints in sweltering heat or busting through tackles for touchdowns. "The way he talked to me, it really, really pissed me off," Lott said. "That's when my animosity for Texas started."

Lott ended up signing with OU and was inserted into the starting lineup for Texas week in 1976. The game ended in a 6–6 tie, and from there, anticipation for the '77 rematch mounted. After beating Ohio State in Columbus, the Sooners were ranked second; behind Earl Campbell, Texas was fifth. "I feel a lot more confident and a lot more relaxed this time," Lott would say. "I can't wait." But Texas had the best defense in the country, and the Longhorns completely stifled Lott and the wishbone. OU had less than 150 yards rushing midway through the fourth quarter, and trailed 13–6 after Russell Erxleben's 58-yard field goal. With six minutes left, the Sooners had one final chance to crack the Texas front lines. Lott completed a pass for 10 yards. David Overstreet rushed for 15 on a pitchout. The Sooners, finally, were in overdrive. "We started running the option again, and moved right down the field," Lott said. "I thought we were going to score and win the game."

After Kenny King dashed for 14 up the middle, the Sooners were within striking distance of a game-tying touchdown. Then the drive sputtered. After a pair of four-yard runs, Elvis Peacock gained only one on the third-down pitch from Lott, setting up fourth-and-inches from inside the Texas 5.

After faking the dive, Lott went left. With middle linebacker Lance Taylor taking a wide angle, Lott tried to cut back inside. But as he did Taylor just got a piece of Lott's thigh with his left arm to slightly slow him down. Before he could make another move, Lott was met by All-Americans Brad Shearer and Johnnie Johnson for no gain. "Once I saw the hole, I was getting ready to dive forward," Lott said. "But as I planted my feet, I couldn't move. If [Shearer] and I had met, just me and him, there's no way in the world he would have stopped me. I would have gotten that yard. I was stronger than he was." Instead, Texas took over possession and prevailed 13–6. "That day was one of the top three worst days of my life," Lott said. "It was a really upsetting football game for me."

All Lott wanted to do was get home. Before heading to the bus, he stopped to chat with his family, who had driven up from San Antonio for the game. But when Lott went to where the bus had been waiting, he found it had already departed. "The game is completely eating me up, and now the bus is gone," Lott said. "My family is gone, they think I'm on my way back to Oklahoma. And the team thinks I'm with my family."

Security tried to taxi Lott to the airport to meet the team there. But Cotton Bowl traffic prevented him from arriving before the Sooners' flight left. Instead, Lott had to wait for the next flight to Oklahoma City, which was chock-full of OU fans. Lott tried to hide in the bar. But his patented bandana was a dead giveaway. Gradually, the whole plane came over to talk to *the* Thomas Lott. "For the next hour, I have to sit there, be cordial, and swallow how I'm really feeling until I get to Norman," said Lott, who would finish his Red River career with a win in '78. "All the way around, just a terrible day."

TEXAS CONFERENCE CHAMPIONSHIPS (32)

Big 12 Conference

2009, 2005 (Mack Brown)

1996 (John Mackovic)

Southwest Conference

1995, 1994 (John Mackovic)

1990 (David McWilliams)

1983, 1977 (Fred Akers)

1975, 1973, 1972, 1971, 1970, 1969, 1968, 1963, 1962, 1961, 1959
(Darrell Royal)

1953, 1952 (Ed Price)

1950 (J. Blair Cherry)

1945, 1943, 1942 (D.X. Bible)

1930, 1928 (Clyde Littlefield)

1920 (Berry Whitaker)

1918 (Bill Juneau)

1916 (Eugene Van Gent)

Texas Intercollegiate Athletic Association

1914, 1913 (Dave Allerdice)

T E X A S

SOONERS SAIL SNAP

This one was different. This one was personal. And the Sooners had a chance to win it. If only they could have converted an extra-point snap.

In the days leading up to the 1976 OU-Texas game, Darrell Royal, who had lost five straight to Barry Switzer, publicly accused the Sooners coach of spying on his practices. Royal went so far as to challenge Switzer, assistant Larry Lacewell, and the alleged spy, Lonnie Williams, to take lie-detector tests

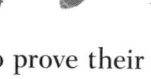

to prove their innocence. If they passed, Royal would donate $10,000 to the charity of their choice. The day before the game, Switzer answered that it was "worth more money to me to have him look for ghosts."

During the pregame warm-ups, Royal and Switzer avoided each other. Gerald Ford attended the game and walked between the two coaches to midfield for the coin toss. On the way, Royal and Switzer refused to acknowledge one another, creating a tense situation for the president.

The game, however, failed to live up to its hype. Featuring a vanilla scheme with inexperienced quarterback Thomas Lott, who had replaced an ill Dean Blevins that week, OU managed just 34 yards of total offense the entire first half. The Longhorns offense didn't fare much better. OU's defense was still strong even without a Selmon on its defensive line for the first time in the 1970s.

Texas carried a 6–0 lead into the fourth quarter courtesy of a pair of Russell Erxleben field goals. But with 5:31 to play, reserve OU tackle David Hudgens swiped the ball out of the arms of running back Ivey Suber, and Sooners safety Zac Henderson pounced on the fumble at the UT 37. The Sooners had done zip offensively all game, with only two first downs. Yet all of a sudden, they had a chance to win. After nine painfully short runs, halfback Horace Ivory, a hero in the '75 game, followed lead blocker Elvis Peacock around left end for a one-yard touchdown run with 1:38 remaining.

Uwe von Schamann had proven to be the most reliable place-kicker in Sooners history. But von Schamann never got a

chance to win the game. Just before the snap, UT linebacker Lionell Johnson leaned in and said, "Center, bet you snap it over his head." Sure enough, Kevin Craig's snap sailed high to holder Bud Hebert, who couldn't bring down the ball. Hebert scrambled back 15 yards to scoop up the ball, but his desperate pass into the end zone was intercepted.

"The snap wasn't that bad," Switzer said. "It was a little high, but you got to handle the ball when it's a little high. But that's what happens. It's part of the game. An opportunity we didn't take advantage of." Instead, OU had to settle for the 6–6 tie. "That was one of the worst feelings in the world," Henderson said. "They say a tie is better than a loss. I don't know about that."

After the game, Craig was inconsolable. "Nothing happened— I just snapped it high," he said. "I'll live, I guess. I guess they'll start recruiting centers now." During the postgame press conference, Switzer defended his deep snapper: "It's just one of those things that happened. I'm sure he feels worse about it than anyone in the stadium."

Switzer was right about that. As Craig fought back tears at his locker, Switzer walked up to him and said, "If this is the worst thing that happens to you in the next 70 years, you'll be okay."

SAM BRADFORD GOES DOWN, AGAIN

It was all too excruciatingly familiar for Oklahoma fans. Quarterback Sam Bradford flushed out of the pocket and planted into the ground, shoulder first. This time, though, Bradford wouldn't be back.

The season before, in 2008, Bradford lit the college football world on fire, lighting up college football defenses along the way. After setting the freshman NCAA record with 36 touchdown passes in '07, Bradford engineered one of the great offensive seasons in college football history in '08. He threw for a school-record 50 touchdowns and 4,720 yards, as the Sooners became the first team in 104 years to total more than 700 points in a season. OU led the nation in scoring, averaging more than 51 points a game, and closed the Big 12 season by scoring 60 points in five straight games, another FBS record. Bradford won the Heisman Trophy, and OU advanced to the BCS title game before falling short to Florida.

Coming off such a spectacular season, most people believed that Bradford would forego his junior season and enter the NFL Draft. Many pundits, in fact, rated Bradford the top draft-eligible quarterback. Instead, Bradford bucked the trend and announced he was coming back to college. Tight end Jermaine Gresham, offensive tackle Trent Williams, and defensive tackle Gerald McCoy—who would all be future first-round draft picks—followed Bradford's lead and elected to return, too. What was looking like a team about to go into rebuilding mode was suddenly primed to make another run at the title.

All of that, however, was not to be. What seemed like a potential dream season quickly turned into a nightmare in the opener against Brigham Young in Cowboys Stadium. In the closing minutes of the first half, as Bradford rolled right to pass, linebacker Coleby Clawson popped Bradford and drove his shoulder into the turf . Bradford had to be helped off the field, his throwing shoulder severely sprained. Without

Sooners QB Sam Bradford is driven to the turf by Texas cornerback Aaron Williams in the first half of the Red River Shootout in 2009. Bradford suffered a season-ending injury to his right shoulder, and the Sooners lost 16–13.

Bradford or Gresham—who earlier that week had suffered a season-ending knee injury—the Sooners were stunned 14–13.

A month later, Bradford returned to the lineup and led OU to a 33–7 win over Baylor. The national championship dreams had already been ended. But the Sooners could still vie for a third consecutive Big 12 title with Bradford back at quarterback—especially if they could get past their next opponent, the third-ranked Longhorns.

On the opening drive, the recharged Sooners looked up to the challenge. DeMarco Murray caught a Bradford screen pass and followed a cavalry of blockers 64 yards, setting up a short

field goal. But that would be Bradford's final completion wearing a Sooners uniform.

The first play of OU's next drive, Texas called the cornerback blitz. As Bradford faked a handoff, he turned his head, only to see Aaron Williams crashing down on him. After the hit, Bradford immediately grabbed for his right shoulder while writhing on the ground. No one on the crimson side of the 50 said a word. But they all had to be thinking the same thing. "You felt the air deflate out of everyone," said linebacker Ryan Reynolds.

The OU defense gave a gutsy performance to keep the Sooners in the game with freshman quarterback Landry Jones. But it wasn't enough, as OU fell short, 16–13. The next week, Bradford announced he was undergoing season-ending surgery and would be declaring for the draft. OU ended up with five losses that season, the most since Bob Stoops' first year.

WORSTER PLOWS FORWARD

In the spring of 1968, Darrell Royal faced a dilemma. He had three outstanding ball carriers in Chris Gilbert, Ted Koy, and Steve Worster. But the Longhorns' wing-T offense called for only two running backs. Wanting to get all three runners on the field at once, Royal charged top assistant Emory Bellard to come up with something.

Bellard's idea was to place the quarterback under center, Worster a foot behind him at fullback, and Gilbert and Koy split behind Worster, making a Y. The formation was called the wishbone-T. And it changed college football forever.

John Brantley Jr., the last quarterback at Florida to run the wishbone, would call the fullback key to running the offense successfully. "If you had a tough fullback," he once told the *Orlando Sentinel*, "they had to take him seriously and couldn't cheat to the outside." In Worster, Texas had such a fullback. "Take away Worster," quarterback James Street would say, "and the wishbone-T becomes nothing but another broke bone."

In its infancy, the 'bone already looked broken. The Horns tied Houston, then got walloped the following week at Texas Tech. But against OU, the it finally came together. The week of the game, Bellard and Royal determined that Worster had been playing too close to the quarterback, and needed to be an extra half-yard back to get going. Such a small tweak would make a huge difference. And against the Sooners, the wishbone-T would be vindicated.

The Longhorns trailed 20–19 at their own 15 with only 2:37 remaining. But Street marched the Horns to the OU 21 with four big completions, setting up Worster's heroics. Well within range, Royal was simply angling for a field-goal try. Instead, Worster rumbled 14 yards to the OU 7. With the orange-bloods hollering, "Woo! Woo!" Royal called Worster's number again. Off right guard, Worster ran over over one Sooner, then another, then another, before dragging two tacklers across the goal line for the game-winning score with 39 seconds left. "We had played so well," said tight end Steve Zabel, who was asked the next week to go both ways to help OU's middling defense. "It was just a crushing lost."

Worster's run solidified the wishbone as a viable attack among reporters, players, and fans, buoying Texas to a 30-game

winning streak that included the 1969 national championship. After enduring 11 losses to Texas in 12 years, OU installed Bellard's wishbone two years later at the prodding of budding assistant Barry Switzer.

OU RUNS OUT

Oklahoma dominated Texas every which way in 1990. The Sooners nearly tripled the Horns in rushing yards, forced twice as many turnovers, and controlled the field position. In fact, Texas penetrated the OU 40-yard line just once before the final four minutes of the fourth quarter.

But the outcome was determined by one critical area that didn't appear in the box score. When the game was on the line, Texas put its fate in the hands of its quarterback. The Sooners, well, not so much.

OU began the season with modest expectations. The Sooners had lost four games the year before and had major questions on either side of the ball, especially at quarterback, as the program had abandoned the triple option. Adding to the gloomy outlook, the Sooners remained on probation and would be ineligible for a bowl for the second consecutive year.

That gloom, however, rapidly turned to optimism. OU opened with a 20-point win at No. 19 UCLA. Then the Sooners hammered No. 13 Pittsburgh, Tulsa, Kansas, and Oklahoma State, propelling them all the way up to No. 4 in the polls. Gary Gibbs' move to swipe Oklahoma State offensive coordinator Larry Coker away in the off-season was proving to be ingenious. Through five games, OU surprisingly had one of the top

scoring teams in the country, even though Coker had yet to settle on either wishbone remnant Steve Collins or blue-chip freshman passer Cale Gundy at quarterback. Even without the opportunity for a bowl game, the Sooners suddenly were serious title contenders going into the Cotton Bowl, where they were 8½-point favorites over unranked Texas.

For most of the day, the game had the makings of an all-time OU defensive performance. Led by linebacker Joe Bowden, the Sooners handcuffed quarterback and '89 Red River hero Peter Gardere while obliterating the Texas ground game. With 7:12 left in the fourth quarter, UT had managed only six first downs and 141 yards of offense.

OU's offense, however, failed to cash in on the defensive effort. In the second quarter, Coker subbed in Gundy for an ineffective Collins, who had completed just one of five passes. But, instead of unleashing the arm of the former *Parade* All-American, Coker called 29 consecutive running plays and ran the ball five times on third-and-long. "If you're going to be a national champion," Gundy told reporters after the game, "you have to throw the football more."

Even with the perplexing play-calling, OU needed just one or two more stops to top off the win. Texas, down 13–7, was pinned on its own 9-yard line and in need of a touchdown, and quickly.

"It was looking down and dismal for us," Texas split end Johnny Walker would say. "It looked like we were out of the game. We had been just dominated to that point." But, as the *Fort Worth Star-Telegram*'s Whit Canning put it, the Sooners

"had sadly underestimated Peter the Great and his amazing band of accomplices."

Out of nowhere, freshman running back Butch Hadnot, who *had not* touched the ball once, replaced injured starter Phil Brown and responded with runs of 21, 16, and two yards. The Sooners aided UT's cause by committing a face mask penalty, then getting flagged for defensive pass interference on a third-down incompletion. "It was kind of déjà vu," said Gardere, who led UT to a game-winning touchdown drive over OU the year before. The Sooners had the same ominous feeling.

On fourth-and-7 at the 16, Gardere noticed OU slide a safety over to help with Walker, who had caught the game-winning pass from Gardere the year before. Gardere coolly read the defense and zipped a strike to Keith Cash the other way for the go-ahead touchdown. "They moved the safety over, so I knew Keith would be open on a short crossing pattern," Gardere said. "When he had to put everything together, we did."

The Sooners still had two minutes to get in range for a game-winning field goal. Surely they would try to pass their way there, right? On fourth-and-8, Gundy scrambled right and found Ted Long for a 17-yard diving catch to the UT 46. Then, with still a minute to work with, Gundy completed another crossing pass to the 35. One more completion, and place-kicker R.D. Lashar would be well within range. Only the Sooners inexplicably wouldn't call another pass. To Gundy's disbelief, Coker called three straight runs up the middle for a total gain of six yards, and instead of using his final timeout, Gibbs rushed Lashar onto the field for a 46-yard try as time was expiring. "I think

they felt comfortable with R.D. kicking," Gundy said. "Shoot, it's always different in hindsight. Obviously, you would have liked to get a few more yards. But obviously they felt, 'We're in position here, we've got a good kicker, let's not continue to put the pressure on an 18-year-old freshman quarterback. So, if he doesn't turn the ball over, we have a chance to win the game. Let's do that.'" Instead, Lashar's kick sailed wide right, and Texas won 14–13.

Afterward, in the dressing room, that 18-year-old freshman told anyone who would listen that he thought his coaches had been too conservative, especially on the failed scoring drive. "I would have preferred to have thrown more passes, but our coaches wanted to run some draws," Gundy said to reporters. "That doesn't seem like much of a two-minute offense to me."

ALLEN STONE-COLD STOPPED

In Austin, they call it the "Stone Cold Stop." But in reality, it was Texas linebacker Robert Reed who facilitated Stonie Clark's infamous goal-line stonewall of James Allen.

Trailing 17–10 in the final minutes, Oklahoma took possession with one last chance after UT's Phil Dawson missed a 48-yard field goal. OU quarterback Garrick McGee hit tight end Stephen Alexander for 11 yards, then found wideout P.J. Mills for 41. Three plays later, the Sooners had first-and-goal from the UT 6.

Fullback Jerald Moore went off tackle to the 3. The Sooners then called another pass, but it was nearly intercepted. On third

TEXAS

TEXAS' NATIONAL CHAMPIONSHIP SEASONS

Year	Record	Coach
1963	11–0	Darrell Royal
1969	11–0	Darrell Royal
1970	10–1	Darrell Royal
2005	13–0	Mack Brown

down, McGee scrambled back to the line of scrimmage, setting up fourth-and-goal from the 3 and the "Stone Cold Stop."

"The [coaches] kept telling me, 'You're not going to make those plays on the other side of the field. The best thing for you to do is stay home, wait for a cutback, or wait for a reverse,'" Reed would say. "That's what I did."

Lucky for the Longhorns he did. With 43 seconds to go, OU offensive coordinator Watson Brown [Mack's younger brother] called a wingback reverse for Allen to the left. A gutsy call that would have worked—had Reed not stayed home. "I was waiting on him. Our eyes met. He started throwing all these jukes. Time stood still. Things started going in slow motion," Reed said. "I wanted to make the tackle, or at worst, make him run where my posse is. If he gets to the corner, it's six and we lose. I hit his leg. I saw him trip."

Before Allen could regather his footing, Clark and his 340-pound frame came barreling down on him, and the train

wreck occurred a foot away from the goal line. "If Robert hadn't gotten to him, [Allen] would have scored," Clark would say. "As soon as I saw Robert turn him back inside, I knew I had a chance to make the play. It was the most memorable play I've ever made in my whole life."

The play sent OU into a tailspin. The Sooners finished 6–6, and coach Gary Gibbs, who dropped to 1–5 against Texas, was fired before OU was blown out in the Copper Bowl.

For Allen, the moment was as unforgettable as it was for Clark, but for the opposite reason. "Just being stopped like that and shouldering all that, that was a lot—a lot for me to handle," Allen said. "But coach Brown told me afterward, 'Trust me, one day, you're going to get them back. You're going to get your due.'" Two years later, Allen would.

POISONED AND PICKED

The 1959 season began under the most ominous of circumstances for quarterback Bobby Boyd and the Sooners. In Bud Wilkinson's first meeting against a Big Ten opponent, Oklahoma traveled to play Ara Parseghian's Northwestern Wildcats, who had defeated both Ohio State and Michigan the year before.

Wilkinson flew the Sooners to Evanston a couple of days early and treated the team to dinner Thursday night at the Chez Paree night club, where the likes of Frank Sinatra, Sammy Davis Jr., and Bob Hope performed regularly. That night, Patrice Wymore was slated to sing. But what was supposed to be a relaxing evening turned into a nightmare. After

eating the fruit salad, many of the players came down with food poisoning. "I remember going into the restroom, and there were so many people in there vomiting, it must have been heel deep," halfback Brewster Hobby would say. "We were just piled on top of each other." Several had to be rushed to the hospital to get their stomachs pumped, including Boyd, who got so sick he had to be strapped to a hospital bed.

Earlier that very same day, the betting line had moved three points, raising suspicion the second-ranked Sooners had been poisoned. Sports information director Harold Keith surmised that Chicago mobsters, who frequented the Chez Paree, had infiltrated the club and poisoned the players. But no one, including a passive Chicago police force, could prove what happened. Two days later in a driving rainstorm, the sickly Sooners were destroyed on national television and plummeted out of the rankings for the first time in eight years.

Two weeks later, OU was back in the national spotlight with a chance to salvage its season against the fourth-ranked Longhorns. After falling behind early, the Horns roared back to recapture a 19–12 lead in the fourth quarter. Twice OU would drive into UT territory with a chance to tie the game. But twice, Boyd would be intercepted, with the final pick proving to be the defining play.

With time dwindling away, the Sooners were on the move and, after a pair of first downs, were within striking distance of the end zone. But on Boyd's next pass, he overthrew Dick Carpenter by just a couple of inches, and UT's Mike Cotten, the culprit in allowing OU's first two touchdowns, made him pay dearly with a diving interception at

the 8-yard line. Texas ran out the clock to seal its second straight win in the rivalry.

"If Boyd had connected, it possibly would have been a touchdown, since Carpenter was in the open and Texas in no position to make a defensive play," Wilkinson would say. "It's just those inches that decide the game." And, once or twice, food poisoning.

STENSRUD CRASHES INTO KING

Coach Jim Mackenzie's first recruiting class proved to be one of the best in Oklahoma history. End Steve Zabel, linebacker Jim Files, and fullback Steve Owens all became first-round draft picks, an OU record that would not be broken until 2010. But in their three years on the field, the recruiting class of 1966 could never beat Texas.

"We could have easily won all three, too," Zabel said. "It's a sad thing for me and my teammates. When I go to reunions with guys that played on other teams, most of those guys beat Texas, and a lot of them beat Texas three or four times. When they start talking, I have to shut up and take my medicine. No matter how old I get, that thorn is still in my side."

The '69 game was as painful as the rest. Texas was ranked second, nipping at the heels of defending national champion Ohio State. The triple-threat of quarterback James Street, fullback Steve Worster, and split end Cotton Speyrer was as imposing as any in college football. But the Sooners, coming off two impressive wins over Wisconsin and Pittsburgh, countered with a stout backfield of their own. Owens would win the

Heisman in '69, and sophomore quarterback Jack Mildren had been the No. 1 recruit in the nation. "It will be an old-fashioned, country, jaw-to-jaw, knucks-down gut check," said UT coach Darrell Royal, who went on to explain what "knucks-down" meant. "Yeah, like when you shot marbles as a kid and then you started playing 'keeps,' and everybody got knucks down, and you hoped the other guy's hand would quiver, and if it didn't, you knew you were all covered up with trouble."

OU-TEXAS STARTING QBs SINCE 1970

Year	Oklahoma	Texas
1970	Jack Mildren	Eddie Phillips
1971	Jack Mildren	Donn Wiggington
1972	Dave Robertson	Alan Lowry
1973	Steve Davis	Marty Akins
1974	Steve Davis	Marty Akins
1975	Steve Davis	Marty Akins
1976	Thomas Lott	Mike Cordaro
1977	Thomas Lott	Mark McBath
1978	Thomas Lott	Donnie Little
1979	J.C. Watts	Donnie Little
1980	J.C. Watts	Donnie Little
1981	Kelly Phelps	Rick McIvor
1982	Kelly Phelps	Robert Brewer
1983	Danny Bradley	Rob Moerschell
1984	Danny Bradley	Todd Dodge
1985	Troy Aikman	Todd Dodge
1986	Jamelle Holieway	Bret Stafford
1987	Jamelle Holieway	Bret Stafford
1988	Jamelle Holieway	Shannon Kelley
1989	Tink Collins	Peter Gardere

TEXAS

The Sooners didn't quiver and actually landed the first punches. Mildren faked a pitch to halfback Roy Bell, then cut back behind Bell's block for the first touchdown. Two possessions later, after a Texas turnover, Owens leaped over a block by left guard Steve Tarlton across the goal line. OU 14, Texas 0. "Not only that, the Sooners, with Steve Owens churning over everything in his path and young Jack Mildren looking as cool as if he had been born in the Cotton Bowl, suggested that they

Year	Oklahoma	Texas
1990	Steve Collins	Peter Gardere
1991	Cale Gundy	Peter Gardere
1992	Cale Gundy	Peter Gardere
1993	Cale Gundy	Shea Morenz
1994	Garrick McGee	James Brown
1995	Eric Moore	James Brown
1996	Justin Fuente	James Brown
1997	Justin Fuente	James Brown
1998	Brandon Daniels	Major Applewhite
1999	Josh Heupel	Major Applewhite
2000	Josh Heupel	Major Applewhite
2001	Nate Hybl	Chris Simms
2002	Nate Hybl	Chris Simms
2003	Jason White	Chance Mock
2004	Jason White	Vince Young
2005	Rhett Bomar	Vince Young
2006	Paul Thompson	Colt McCoy
2007	Sam Bradford	Colt McCoy
2008	Sam Bradford	Colt McCoy
2009	Sam Bradford	Colt McCoy
2010	Landry Jones	Garrett Gilbert
2011	Landry Jones	Case McCoy

TEXAS

might be capable of doing it all afternoon," wrote Dan Jenkins of *Sports Illustrated*.

Behind repeated bombs from Street to Speyrer, Texas came roaring back and led 20–17 in the fourth quarter. But Mildren started to catch fire again, completing three passes, as OU drove 50 yards to the Texas 27. An offside penalty and subsequent missed field goal ended the drive. But there was enough time for Mildren and company to get another chance. Or so they thought.

With just a few minutes left, OU forced another UT punt. Glenn King was back to field the return, while teammate Bruce Stensrud stood 10 yards in front of him. As the ball fluttered against the wind like a knuckleball, Stensrud backpedaled and signaled for a fair catch. But King didn't see Stensrud and waited for the ball to come to him. Stensrud, Texas cover man Jim Bertelsen, and the ball all arrived in King's lap at once, sending the ball flying. UT's Bob McKay fell on it a the OU 23, and Worster, who had scored the game-winning touchdown the year before, broke Sooners hearts again with a one-yard plunge to ice this one 27–17. "We hadn't had anybody jump right down our throats before. They were on us like white on rice, and that's completely covered," Royal would say. "The statistics show it was an even game. The big difference was that fumbled punt."

Spurred by the win, UT went on to capture the school's second national championship, beating Notre Dame 21–17 in the Cotton Bowl. The Sooners' season went the other direction. After losses to Kansas State, Missouri, and Nebraska, OU was just 5–4 heading into the finale at Oklahoma State. Bum-

per stickers had been showing up around the state that read, "chuck Chuck." But a week after winning the Heisman Trophy, Owens responded with one of the great individual performances in Sooners history. He rushed for 261 yards and two touchdowns on 55 carries, as OU held on to win 28–27 to salvage its season. "I'm almost positive Chuck Fairbanks would have gotten fired, along with the whole staff, had we not beaten Oklahoma State," Zabel said.

Instead, OU kept Fairbanks and assistant Barry Switzer, and the following year Switzer would install the wishbone offense that launched the Sooners' second dynasty.

3

RED RIVER VILLAINS WE HATE

PETER GARDERE

Near the end of his fourth and—mercifully for Oklahoma—final Red River Rivalry game quarterbacking the Longhorns, Peter Gardere was on the sideline celebrating victory with his teammates. In the stands, a pocket of Sooners fans began chanting, "Graduate! Graduate!" Gardere finally did. But not before becoming the first and only quarterback on either side of the rivalry to go 4–0 as a starter in the series. "I'm just glad I snuck one out my senior year," said OU quarterback Cale Gundy, who lost to Gardere three times before leading the Sooners to victory after he had graduated in '93. "I don't know if I could have stayed in this state had I not beat Texas. I'm glad I'm not one of them who went 0–4."

Gardere did not possess the talent of Bobby Layne, James Street, or, most definitely, Vince Young. He was just 25–16 as a starter and played through a pair of losing seasons. But every time he suited up against the Sooners, Gardere morphed into "Peter the Great."

"I didn't do it myself," said Gardere, whose father and grandfather also quarterbacked the Horns. "We had some

low-scoring games where the defense did everything, and we didn't do much on offense at all." Good luck convincing Sooner Nation. His first two outings, Gardere broke OU's heart with game-winning, come-from-behind, fourth-quarter touchdown drives. And in his final appearance, Peter the Perfect broke OU's back with a then–Texas series record 274 passing yards. Not only did Gardere lead the Horns to four consecutive wins, but in each case Texas entered unranked and the underdog. The Sooners, conversely, came in ranked No. 15, No. 4, No. 6, and No. 16.

The week before the '89 OU game, Gardere broke into the starting lineup as a freshman and rallied Texas past Rice— a precursor of what was to come in the Cotton Bowl. Texas trailed OU late, but Gardere completed all five of his passes on the final drive, including the game-winning, 25-yard touchdown strike to Johnny Walker.

The following year it was the same Gardere, second verse. On fourth-and-7 from the OU 16, Gardere found tight end Keith Cash breaking free over the middle for yet another game-winning touchdown. The next two meetings, all Gardere had to do was play his game and allow the Texas' defense to dominate. The Longhorns won 10–7 in '91, then 34–24 in '92 in a game that wasn't nearly as close as the final margin indicated. By then, UT fans had another nickname for Gardere: "Four-Pete."

"My other records will be broken," Gardere said afterward, "but this is how I hope to be remembered." To this day, Gardere is remembered for two things: as James Van Der Beek's

quarterback double in the film *Varsity Blues*, and as the quarterback OU couldn't beat.

BOBBY LAYNE

In Detroit, it's known as the Curse of Bobby Layne. After Layne led the Lions to a third NFL championship, Detroit traded its franchise quarterback to Pittsburgh in 1958. In response, legend has it Layne said the Lions would not win for 50 years. Cursed, Detroit has endured through the worst winning percentage of any NFL team over the last 50 years and has yet to play for another championship. But the Lions weren't the only ones to be cursed by the "Blond Bomber."

Layne grew up in Dallas and played high school ball at Highland Park with the great Doak Walker, who would star at SMU before teaming up with Layne again in Detroit. "Bobby Layne never lost a game. Time just ran out," Walker once said. "Nobody hated to lose more than Bobby."

Nobody loved having fun more than Layne, either. After convincing him to come to Austin, UT coach Dana X. Bible

TEXAS

TEXAS' HEISMAN TROPHY WINNERS

Player	Position	Year
Earl Campbell	RB	1977
Ricky Williams	RB	1998

couldn't wait to see what Layne could do. Bible would have to wait another day. Layne didn't show up for the first practice. When Bible asked where he was, Layne answered, "Coach, you don't even want to know."

Like fellow UT quarterback James Street, the hard-partying, hard-drinking Layne doubled as a star pitcher for the UT baseball team. Once, while pitching a no-hitter against Texas A&M, Layne drank 10 beers in the dugout to kill the pain in his foot, which he cut open partying the night before. When asked how he could party all night, then play so well the next day, Layne replied, "I sleep fast."

It wasn't long before Bible charged 4'11" Rooster Andrews, the team's water boy/kicker, to keep Layne out of trouble. Late one night during Layne's first season at Austin, he woke Andrews up with a random question: "When you're back there drop-kicking on extra points, I wonder if we could fake the thing and you could throw it to me on the left flat?" The two would successfully unleash the play against the Sooners that season, but only after the 17-year-old Layne had already thrown two touchdowns. UT won the game 20–0.

Layne missed the '45 meeting with OU—which the Horns won anyway, 12–7—while serving in the Merchant Marines. But in '46, he returned to the rivalry with a vengeance. Outdueling OU's backfield combo of Darrell Royal and Jack Mitchell, Layne scored a touchdown in the first quarter to propel the Longhorns to a 20–13 victory.

The week leading up to the OU game in '47, one AP reporter wrote, "Don't look now, Sooners, but here's that man again.

Yes, Bobby Layne, your old [jinx], will be on deck Saturday. The Oklahoma fans wonder if Bobby is making a career out of beating their football team; he has been around such a long time, or at least it seems that way. As far back as 1944 Bobby was putting the Indian sign on the Sooners. If it is any consolation to Oklahoma, this is Bobby's last year. Next season, everybody can start all over, and Oklahoma may have an even break."

The Sooners would get no breaks in '47 from Layne—or from the officials. With Texas at the OU 2-yard line and only a few seconds remaining before halftime, UT halfback Randall Clay was stopped before the goal line. Official Jack Sisco initially signaled "touchdown," then changed it to "timeout" when it became obvious the Longhorns hadn't scored. Sooners fans screamed that the half was over, but Texas was given one more play—a play that would live in Oklahoma infamy.

As Layne handed off to halfback Jimmy Canady, the ball squirted into the backfield. What happened next remains in dispute. The ball came into Layne's hands while he faced the end zone. Crouching, Layne spun around and pitched the ball to Clay, who then ran around the end for a touchdown. OU coach Bud Wilkinson and his players protested that Layne's knee had been down. But officials let the play stand. The touchdown gave Texas a 14–7 lead and immense momentum heading into the locker room. Years later, on the matter of whether his knee was down, Layne would say, "To tell you the truth, I promise you I don't know myself to this day. The film didn't show it. Really and truly I don't know, because of the heat of the ballgame, whether I had my knee down or not. I couldn't tell you."

The Longhorns went on to win 34–14, and after several more controversial calls in the second half, OU fans began hurling hundreds of bottles and seat cushions onto the field. The game became known in Oklahoma as the "Sisco Game." But in the dressing room, OU All-America center John Rapacz acknowledged the No. 1 reason why they hadn't won. "It's the same old story," he said. "We play our hearts out, and that Layne beats us."

JAMES STREET AND COTTON SPEYRER

Before Colt McCoy and Jordan Shipley, there was James Street and Cotton Speyrer. And, as with McCoy and Shipley, the Sooners had little answer for either.

Street was a quarterback cut from the same quilt as predecessor Bobby Layne. Before enrolling at Texas, Street traveled to Hershey, Pennsylvania, with 32 other Texans for a high school all-star game against the best from the Keystone State. The coaches from each side had agreed that there would be no blitzing. But in the game, Texas blitzed on almost every play and wiped out the Pennsylvanians. The coach of that Texas squad? Bobby Layne. The Blond Bomber never lost to Oklahoma. Neither would Street. "Whatever was called, you just felt it was going to work because of the attitude James brought," UT halfback Ted Koy would say. "He had that infectious optimism."

Speyrer, who grew up in Joe Washington's hometown of Port Arthur, Texas, brought the same cocksure attitude to the Texas huddle. When Speyrer tried out for eighth-grade football at Woodrow Wilson, the coaches told him he was too gaunt to play. Speyrer convinced them to give him a uniform,

and he finally got to touch the ball after replacing the team's star player on the final play of a game. Speyrer sped 50 yards for a touchdown and never left the field again. "Boy, he could run," said Washington, who idolized Speyrer as a kid. "Slight, but an unbelievable athlete."

In the spring of '68, neither Street nor Speyrer were starters. And coach Darrell Royal had given neither much thought. Royal was more concerned with how to get his three outstanding runners—Koy, Chris Gilbert, and Steve Worster—on the field at the same time. At Royal's behest, assistant Emory Bellard devised the wishbone-T offense, which would ultimately fuel the Horns to 30 consecutive wins and the 1969 national championship. First, though, Royal had to find the right conductor.

The '68 season got off to a horrible start. Texas tied Houston, then fell behind at Texas Tech 28–6. Desperate, Royal benched two-year starting quarterback Bill Bradley and inserted Street. "Get in there," Royal told Street. "Hell, you can't do any worse." At first glance, playing Street at all seemed to be foolhardy. Street was a star pitcher, whose first sport was baseball. But the substitution proved to be genious. The wishbone had sputtered because Bradley, who later found his calling at defensive back, attempted to turn every play into a big one. Street understood the wishbone was meant to grind out its opponents—then pop the big play. Street gave the Horns the spark they needed and nearly rallied them from the 22-point deficit. Royal had his conductor.

Two weeks after taking over the reins, Street faced a defining moment in his career. The Horns trailed OU 20–19 with only

TOP 5 TEXAS RECEIVING GAMES vs. OU

1. **Cotton Speyrer** | 160 yards | 1969
   8 catches, 1 TD | 27–17 (Texas)

2. **Wane McGarity** | 153 yards | 1998
   6 catches, 1 TD | 34–3 (Texas)

3. **Jermichael Finley** | 149 yards | 2007
   4 catches, 1 TD | 28–21 (OU)

4. **Quan Cosby** | 122 yards | 2008
   9 catches | 45–35 (Texas)

5. **Mike Adams** | 117 yards | 1993
   7 catches, 2 TDs | 38–17 (OU)

TEXAS

2:37 to play and the ball at their own 15-yard line. The wishbone was not designed to come from behind with the pass. But it would this day. On the first play, Street rolled out, then threw back to tight end Deryl Comer for an 18-yard completion. Against OU's prevent defense, Street found Comer for 21 yards and again for 13. Then he smoked a pass to Bradley, who had moved to split end, to the Sooners 21. Suddenly, the Horns were in field-goal range. But they wouldn't need to attempt one. On two carries, Worster plowed his way into the end zone with 39 seconds remaining, handing the Horns an improbable victory. The wishbone was solidified, with Street as its maestro. Texas did not lose again the rest of the regular season, and was invited back to the Cotton Bowl to play Tennessee. After UT won the pregame coin toss, the referee asked

Street whether the Horns wanted to kick, receive, or defend a goal. To which Street responded, "We really don't give a damn." The Horns rolled 36–13.

The following season, Street broke Sooners hearts again— only this time, with Speyrer supplying the downfield damage. Even though Texas was a heavy favorite, the Sooners jumped to an early 14–0 lead behind the ramrod running of Steve Owens and clever ball-handling of an up-and-coming sophomore quarterback named Jack Mildren. OU had also been gambling, successfully, by placing eight defenders in the box to stop Worster and company from running wild. After the Sooners' second touchdown, Street turned to Speyrer and said, "Get ready to start catching the ball."

Before the game, Royal had shrewdly declared that the difference between the two teams might be the defensive backfields. "We're zone. They're man-to-man. I don't believe they can cover Speyrer one-on-one." Royal was never more right. On the first play of UT's ensuing drive, Street zoomed a pass 35 yards downfield to Speyrer, who made a leaping catch. OU stuck with its eight-man front. So Street lobbed another throw Speyrer's way, a 24-yard score that Speyrer pulled down over OU's Bruce Stensrud. "We didn't anticipate Cotton Speyrer running as fast as he did," Stensrud said. "He just chewed each one of us up."

When the chewing was done, Speyrer had eight catches, 160 yards, and the touchdown. To cope, the Sooners finally had to relinquish crowding the box, which allowed the UT ground game to get rolling. "Speyrer's jittery presence out there in the OU secondary," wrote *Sports Illustrated*'s Dan Jenkins,

"managed to spread the Sooners too thin, and eventually Texas' own hammering ball carriers, the Steve Worsters, Ted Koys, and Jim Bertelsens, controlled the game." Texas came from behind again, beating the Sooners 27–17.

In the same stadium in the same season, Street connected on a critical fourth-down completion to Speyrer in the final minute, setting up UT's game-winning touchdown over Notre Dame to secure the school's second national championship. The final score "might have been different if Notre Dame's opponent had been a team without a few midgets like James Street and Cotton Speyrer," Jenkins wrote, "who can't do anything but play college football—and can't do anything but win."

TOMMY NOBIS

In 1961, prior to becoming the greatest defender in Texas history, Tommy Nobis briefly considered attending the University of Oklahoma. Nobis had grown up in Texas, listening to Southwest Conference football on the radio. But the Sooners were still the "It" program in college football. OU had won back-to-back national titles just five years earlier. So Nobis accepted a recruiting trip to Norman and met with coach Bud Wilkinson, who took one look at Nobis' oversized neck and tendered him a scholarship offer. Nobis liked what he saw, too.

Then he visited the player dorms, where he ran into a few Texans who had crossed the border to play for the Sooners. "They started talking about the state of Texas and what jerks the people were," Nobis would say. "They were bad-mouthing

the Longhorns and the state of Texas. I couldn't get out of that room fast enough. Once I got my ass across that Red River and into Texas, I didn't go back into Oklahoma. That was an unacceptable situation for me up there. I made up my mind that whether I signed with Texas, Baylor, or Texas A&I, I was going to stay in the state. I was a Texas boy."

A Texas boy who would make life absolutely miserable for Oklahomans. The Sooners put up just 14 points total—all losses—in three games against Nobis, who later called the wins over OU "the best times of my life."

TEXAS NATIONAL AWARD WINNERS

Lombardi (Best Lineman or Linebacker)
Kenneth Sims   1981
Tony Degrate   1984
Brian Orakpo   2008

Butkus (Best Linebacker)
Derrick Johnson   2004

Thorpe (Best Defensive Back)
Michael Huff   2005
Aaron Ross   2006

Davey O'Brien (Best Quarterback)
Vince Young   2005
Colt McCoy   2009

Nagurski (Best Defensive Player)
Derrick Johnson   2004
Brian Orakpo   2008

TEXAS

In 1963 Nobis teamed with tackle Scott Appleton to obliterate OU's offense, 28–7, in the series' first battle of No. 1 vs. No. 2, as Texas went on to win its first national championship. In '64 Nobis recorded 21 tackles as UT stung the Sooners in a game much closer than the 28–7 final score. And in '65 Nobis intercepted a pass early, then recovered a fumble late as UT blanked the Sooners in one of the most dominant defensive performances in the history of the series. OU managed just 114 yards of offense and six first downs that game. The same season, Nobis won the Outland Trophy and earned consensus All-America honors. "He was a tremendous linebacker," said

Walter Camp (Player of the Year)

Ricky Williams	1998
Colt McCoy	2008
Colt McCoy	2009

Maxwell (Player of the Year)

Tommy Nobis	1965
Ricky Williams	1998
Vince Young	2005
Colt McCoy	2009

Doak Walker Award (Best Running Back)

Ricky Williams	1997
Ricky Williams	1998
Cedric Benson	2004

Outland (Best Lineman)

Scott Appleton	1963
Tommy Nobis	1965
Brad Shearer	1977

TEXAS

two-time All-America OU linebacker Carl McAdams, who went head-to-head with Nobis in a pair of epic individual defensive face-offs in '64 and '65. "I felt honored to sometimes be compared in the same sentence as him. I was a little bit leaner, a little faster, and could get to the outside better. But he was bigger, stronger, and could protect the middle better. He was just an outstanding linebacker."

COLT McCOY AND JORDAN SHIPLEY

The most succinct game plan Oklahoma linebacker Keenan Clayton ever saw was the one for Texas. More specifically, the one to stop quarterback Colt McCoy and wide receiver Jordan Shipley. "It was the thinnest playbook we ever used preparing for teams," Clayton said. "They ran the same few plays, year in, year out."

The Sooners knew what McCoy and Shipley were going to do. But more times than not, it still didn't matter. "They didn't have many plays, but they executed them to a T and made plays when they needed to," Clayton said. "I don't know what it was about those guys, but they had a chemistry. A great chemistry."

The unique chemistry shared by McCoy and Shipley went back to their fathers. Brad McCoy and Bob Shipley roomed together as football teammates at Abilene Christian in the early 1980s. In the 1990s Bob Shipley landed a job coaching football at Rotan High School. Twenty miles away, Brad McCoy coached at Hamlin. By the time the two families moved away, the two coaches' sons had become fast friends.

Playing for his dad at Burnet, Jordan Shipley broke Texas state high school records in career receptions, receiving yards, and receiving touchdowns. Playing for his dad at Jim Ned, McCoy became an all-state quarterback and threw for almost 4,000 yards his senior season. Both players were hotly recruited, including Shipley by the Sooners.

But after attending UT's summer football camp together, McCoy and Shipley committed to the Longhorns. They also wound up rooming together, would speak at hospitals and Christian groups together, and would go fishing and hunting together in the summers. "Neither one of us are real loud-type people," Shipley said. "We're pretty easygoing for the most part. We have a good time when we're together, just hanging out." That friendship transferred to remarkable chemistry on the football field, which culminated in perhaps the best quarterback-receiver tandem performance in the history of the Red River Rivalry.

In 2006 McCoy inherited the starting job from Vince Young and was named the Big 12 offensive freshman of the year. Against the Sooners, McCoy delivered one of the coolest Red River debuts for a quarterback since Peter Gardere. He completed 11 of 18 passes for 108 yards and threw a pair of second-half touchdowns, including a seven-yarder to Shipley, as the Longhorns coasted 28–10. McCoy would become even more lethal when Shipley entered the starting lineup two years later.

Going into the 2008 game, few were paying attention to Texas. All eyes were on the Sooners and quarterback Sam Bradford, who was orchestrating the newly installed hurry-up offense with unmatched precision. Even though the Longhorns were

also unbeaten, Vegas favored OU by a touchdown. Early on, it appeared the Sooners might win by five touchdowns.

On scoring drives of 80 and 74 yards, Bradford methodically zipped OU down the field against a bewildered Texas defense. Kicking off up 14–3, the Sooners were within striking distance of effectively putting the game out of reach. "We had 'em down," Clayton said. "We're about to run the score up on 'em." As the coverage team ran onto the field, Clayton and others hollered, "Just get [Shipley] down, we'll do the rest. Just make sure he doesn't run this ball back."

But that's exactly what Shipley did. Taking the ball at the 4, he found an open lane to his right, and sped untouched for the touchdown. "I seen that seam, I knew it was over with," Clayton said. "We had Jamell Fleming on the backside. He was fast enough to go get him, but it was too late. When Shipley cut back, I was like, *Oh, no.* After that it was like an avalanche." Mack Brown would say Shipley's kickoff return "reset the tempo." What it did was give the Longhorns confidence they could win the game.

By halftime, Texas trailed just 21–20. When Ryan Reynolds, OU's middle linebacker and emotional leader, tore his knee up for a third time in his career in the second half, the wind went out of the Sooners' sails. UT offensive coordinator Greg Davis shifted Shipley to tight end, isolating him against Reynolds' untested backup, Brandon Crow. That's when McCoy and Shipley really went to work. Shipley summarily hauled in a one-yard crossing route for a touchdown with Crow trailing him. Then, after OU retook a 35–30 lead in the fourth quarter, Shipley curled in the middle of the field behind an unaware

Texas wide receiver Jordan Shipley scores a touchdown after returning an
Oklahoma kickoff 96 yards in the second quarter of the Longhorns' 45–35
victory in 2008.

Crow. McCoy looked the rest of the defense away, then found
Shipley wide open. With no one behind him, Shipley turned
and raced to the OU 1. On the next play, Texas took the lead
for good, as the Longhorns prevailed 45–35 in the highest-
scoring game in series history. McCoy, who finished his career

with a 3–1 record against the Sooners, completed 28 of 35 passes for 277 yards. Shipley finished with a career-high 11 catches for 112 yards. "They just kept nickeling and diming us," said Reynolds, who could only watch the fourth quarter from the sideline. "They worked great together. They got the matchups with Shipley, and Colt could scramble and make plays out of the pocket."

After taking the Horns to the national championship game in '09, the twosome was finally split up. McCoy was drafted by the Browns; Shipley was taken by the Bengals. But before starting their pro careers, the two had one last hurrah. Shipley was best man in McCoy's wedding, and at the reception, he serenaded his college quarterback with the country song, "I want to be just like Colt McCoy."

STEVE HALL

Barry Switzer once said, "Texas doesn't have to recruit Oklahoma to be successful. Oklahoma *has* to recruit Texas to be successful." But if not for the services of an unheralded Oklahoman, Steve "Two Play" Hall, who knows if Texas would have prevailed over the Sooners twice in the late 1970s?

Hall was a three-sport star at Broken Arrow High School, located in the suburbs of Tulsa. He was all-conference in basketball and track and all-state in football. But plodding tight ends had little usefulness in Switzer's speed-oriented wishbone attack. So when it came time to pick a college in 1977, Hall did the unthinkable. He signed with Texas, where only *one* Oklahoma native had lettered since World War II.

Even though he was a freshman, Hall immediately earned playing time in Austin. The Longhorns needed blockers for workhorse tailback Earl Campbell, and Hall was a blocker.

OU and Texas were loaded in '77. Both teams would be ranked No. 1 at various times during the season. The year before, the rivalry had reached new levels of bitterness because of the feuding between Switzer and Darrell Royal leading up to the game. No one came out satisfied, with the score ending in a 6–6 tie. Both programs and its fans wanted the '77 game. Badly.

After Russell Erxleben and Uwe von Schamann traded field goals, the Longhorns finally put a drive together. Yardage would be precious in this game, as the defenses were stifling. Especially with Billy Sims not playing because of a sore tendon and Texas down to third-string quarterback Randy McEachern after injuries to its first two.

Late in the second quarter, McEachern drove the Horns down the field, thanks to a couple of big completions to split end Alfred Jackson. Facing second-and-9 from the OU 24, the Horns went back to Campbell on a sprint draw. Texas double-teamed nose guard Reggie Kinlaw and blocked OU's Phil Tabor out to the left. Campbell immediately saw the hole open between those two blocks and cut sharply to his left. But the critical block would come upfield.

Campbell ran through Daryl Hunt's arms, then hurdled Barry Burget's diving ankle tackle without breaking stride. Ahead the 215-pound Hall planted his forearms into the chin of

TEXAS PLAYERS IN THE
COLLEGE FOOTBALL HALL OF FAME

Name	Pos.	Years	Inducted
Bobby Layne	QB	1944–1947	1968
Bud Sprague	T	1923–1924	1970
Malcolm Kutner	E	1939–1941	1974
Harrison Stafford	HB	1930–1932	1975
Tommy Nobis	LB/G	1963–1965	1981
Bud McFadin	G	1948–1950	1983
Earl Campbell	RB	1974–1977	1990
Hub Bechtol	E	1944–1946	1991
James Saxton	RB	1959–1961	1996
Chris Gilbert	RB	1966–1968	1999
Harley Sewell	G	1950–1952	2000
Jerry Sisemore	OT	1970–1972	2002
Roosevelt Leaks	RB	1972–1974	2005
Johnnie Johnson	DB	1976–1979	2007
Steve McMichael	DT	1976–1979	2009
Doug English	DT	1972–1974	2011

OU safety Terry Peters, who had broken Jackson's ribs on a hit the year before. "I looked the guy right in the eye and I knew Earl was behind me," Hall would say, "so I went through him." Hall planted Peters back into the turf with a smothering block, clearing the hole for Campbell, who circled to the left before coasting into the end zone. The play would be the only touchdown of the afternoon, as Texas sealed the 13–6 victory with a critical fourth-down stand late. "We had a wonderful line coach named Leon Manley," Hall would later recall. "He

graded the film after the game and came up to me and said, 'I had to give you a double-plus on that play. But I had to give you a minus, too, because you blocked the wrong guy.'"

Two years later in '79, Hall was in the Sooners' craw again. OU took an early 7–3 lead, but late in the half, J.C. Watts was picked off by the Horns, who returned the interception all the way to the Sooners 5. On third-and-goal from the 2, Texas called play-action. "[Lawrence] Sampleton got hurt during the first quarter, so I was running first-string, and Dewey Turner was the second-stringer," Hall said. "We got down to the goal line, and [quarterback] Donnie Little called that play, and it was like, *Oh, my God, that's my play*. So I went up to Dewey after we broke the huddle and told him, 'Get on the other side. This is my play.' We switched, and I went to block the defensive end, fell down, but got up and ran to the corner."

Little faked a handoff to Johnny "Jam" Jones, and lofted a wobbly pass to Hall in the corner of the end zone. Hall outjumped All-America linebacker George Cumby and made a one-handed stab of the pass. Not only was it Hall's first catch in two years, it was believed to be the first Texas touchdown scored by an Oklahoman in the history of the series. "It went about how we had been practicing it," Hall said. "I just faked a block and go out to the end zone. It was a great pass. It is usually open. I really didn't feel like it won the game because we would have won one way or another."

Spurred by the score, the Longhorns went on to a 16–7 victory. No Texas Oklahoman has made as a big impact on the series since.

RUSSELL ERXLEBEN

Russell Erxleben once declared, "Kicking is no fun if you're no good at it." Problem for the Sooners was, Erxleben was good. Maybe the best, in fact.

Erxleben was raised in Seguin, Texas, where his German father was the postmaster. In high school he was equally as good a quarterback as a kicker, and signed with the Longhorns to do both. During his freshman season in '75, he actually considered a transfer to Baylor because he was only kicking. "I didn't know you just kicked," Erxleben would say. "I'd seen guys kick in college, but I just figured they played somewhere else, too." Erxleben soon discovered his sole calling was behind the kicking tee.

In 1976 Erxleben kicked field goals of 37 and 41 yards as Texas tied the Sooners 6–6. Then, the following year, Erxleben put together perhaps the greatest place-kicking season in college football history. The week before the OU game, Erxleben achieved the inconceivable. With the Horns up 54–7 on Rice, UT coach Fred Akers called for a punt with the ball at midfield. Except Erxleben convinced Akers to let him attempt a field goal. Erxleben, also the team's punter, quickly changed into his square-toed place-kicking shoe. He wanted to outdo his buddy, Texas A&M kicker Tony Franklin, who earlier that season had kicked a 65-yard field goal. So Erxleben moved the tee one yard farther back than usual to make it a 67-yarder. With only a slight wind at his back, Erxleben boomed the kick through the middle of the uprights, giving him the longest field goal in NCAA history. "You know what a guy like that does to you?" said OU assistant Larry Lacewell. "He puts you in a goal-line defense on the 50-yard line."

Texas place-kicker Russell Erxleben boots a field goal against Oklahoma in the Longhorns' 13–6 victory in 1977. Erxleben was good from 58 and 64 yards that day.

The Sooners were rightfully worried about Erxleben's kicking prowess going into what figured to be a defensive showdown. All week, Barry Switzer said the UT kicker could be the difference in the game. Erxleben, who during pregame warm-ups thanked Switzer for the "good press," wouldn't disappoint.

That season, OU had its own outstanding kicker of German descent. And Uwe von Schamann, who two weeks earlier had beaten Ohio State with a game-winning kick, gave the Sooners a 3–0 lead over Texas with a 47-yard field goal. For

Erxleben, that seemed like a chip shot. In the second quarter, he countered with a 64-yard bomb, which cleared the crossbar by 10 yards to tie the game. The 64-yarder was the third-longest in NCAA history. "He used this old, beat-up ball for kicking," recalled OU safety Zac Henderson. "That thing looked like it was floating when he kicked it. I always wondered if there was a little helium mixed in with that ball."

The Sooners gave von Schamann a chance to answer with a 63-yard attempt in the second half. The try fell just short, but von Schamann made it 10–6 in the third quarter with a 32-yard make.

But Erxleben—and the Longhorns defense—proved to be too much. After misfiring on a ridiculous 69-yard try, Erxleben nailed a 58-yarder to put the Horns up by a touchdown with eight minutes left. The Texas defense did the rest, stuffing Thomas Lott on fourth-and-short inside the Longhorns 5-yard line to secure UT's first win over the Sooners in seven seasons. "Russell did great," Texas coach Fred Akers would say, "but just what we expected."

The field goals overshadowed the impact Erxleben's punts had in the Longhorns controlling the field-position battle. Erxleben averaged 48.1 yards on nine punts, none more critical than his last one. After the fourth-down stop of Lott, Akers admitted he considered taking a safety so Texas could kick from the 20 instead of its own end zone. Instead, Akers let Erxleben punt, and he responded by launching a 69-yard rocket that effectively put the game away. "With Erxleben, it was like gravity didn't exist," Henderson said. "He was amazing."

JACK CRAIN

Earl Campbell and Ricky Williams might be the two greatest running backs in Texas history. But no back broke Oklahoma's heart more than the "Nocona Nugget."

No UT back had more nicknames than Crain, either. Also called "Jackrabbit Jack" and the "Red Grange of Texas," Crain lived up to those titles when he faced the Sooners.

In 1939 Oklahoma was cruising to victory, ahead 17–0 in the final quarter. With no other recourse, the Horns tossed the stubby-legged, 165-pound Crain into the game. From the Texas 29, Crain took a pitchout on a fake dive play, and torched the Sooners with a 71-yard scoring scamper. On UT's next possession, Crain got the ball on the same play and zipped the same 71 yards down the sideline. All of a sudden, Texas trailed just 17–12. The Sooners had the more experienced team in '39 and marched to a game-clinching score to seal the game. But Crain's antics were a harbinger of what was to come.

In 1940 the power of the rivalry appeared to be swinging north for the first time. The Sooners blanked Texas in '38 before holding on in '39. Only once before had OU beat Texas three straight times, when Bennie Owen's Boomers prevailed in Austin twice, then won the inaugural meeting in Dallas in 1912.

OU had a fine team led by Indian Jack Jacobs, who, until Sam Bradford, remained the only Sooner beside Troy Aikman to attempt a pass in the NFL for six decades. The Creek Indian came out on fire against Texas in 1940, passing and running the Sooners to a 16–7 lead. OU was well on its way to three in

a row. But once again, the Nocona Nugget took over. On virtually the same fake dive play he scored twice on in '39, Crain dashed 63 yards to the OU 2-yard line, setting up a UT touchdown two plays later. Then, in the fourth quarter, the Sooners collapsed. With just five minutes remaining and OU clinging to a 16–13 lead, Cliff Speegle botched the snap to Jacobs on fourth down, handing UT the ball at the OU 12. Crain would make them pay. Three plays later, he zoomed around the left end for the game-winning touchdown.

After being gashed twice, OU's entire game plan the following season centered around containing Crain. By then, it didn't matter. In the 1941 game, Crain hauled in a 26-yard touchdown pass. Then he rushed for an 11-yard score. Crain only carried the ball 10 times in the game. But he still rushed for 144 yards, as UT whitewashed the Sooners 40–7 to capture the inaugural Bronze (now Golden) Hat trophy.

The Red River loss was Snorter Luster's first as OU's coach. He lost the next four and resigned under pressure. To replace Luster, the Sooners hired Jim Tatum, who brought with him a promising assistant named Bud Wilkinson.

All told, Crain, who would later serve in the Texas House of Representatives, finished his three-game Red River career with 353 yards rushing, an average of 13 yards per carry, and five touchdowns.

BUBBA JACQUES

Bubba Jacques broke his word. His entire career, the diminutive defensive back had been telling his Texas teammates that

if he ever scored a touchdown, he would throw the ball into the crowd, 15-yard penalty be damned. Jacques was a diehard Dallas fan and had seen Cowboys wide receiver Drew Pearson do it once. Jacques finally scored that touchdown in the '91 Red River Rivalry. But he wisely opted not to go through with his plan.

After probation and scholarship reductions, Barry Switzer's resignation, and back-to-back losses to Texas, Oklahoma finally seemed to be righting its course in '91. Gary Gibbs, who had replaced Switzer two years earlier, had scrapped the option and signed throwing quarterback Cale Gundy. Through the first four games, the OU aerial show, at least by Sooners standards, was flying high. OU was ranked sixth in the country and had begun to reenter the national title conversations.

But, after a respectable first half against Texas, the Schooner hit the skids. On eight second-half possessions, OU punted six times, was unsuccessful on a fourth down, and lost a costly fumble. That was almost enough to still pull out a victory.

Quarterback Peter Gardere, who led the Horns to fourth-quarter victories the previous two meetings, failed to find his patented Red River rhythm. He completed only 11 of 24 passes, which was only marginally better than Gundy's 5 of 17. As *Sports Illustrated*'s Austin Murphy noted, "Montana vs. Marino this was not."

Yet with Gundy missing passes and Scott Blanton missing field goals (three of them), the Sooners took a 7–3 lead into the fourth quarter. If only they had just taken a knee. Instead, they handed off to fullback Mike McKinley, who was stripped by

Texas tackle James Patton. After whiffing at it twice, Jacques finally scooped up the fumble and raced 30 yards into the end zone. "Just a freak fumble return," Gundy said. Jacques thought for a moment about sticking to his promise. Instead, he dropped the ball to the ground. "I chickened out," Jacques said after the game. "We couldn't afford a 15-yard penalty. We didn't need to be kicking off from the 20."

Truth be told, it would not have mattered. In the final 13 minutes, the Sooners failed to even get in range for a field-goal try before falling 10–7. On their way to the dressing room, the victorious Longhorns walked through the tunnel beneath the scores of downcast Sooners fans still in the stands. Instead of flashing the familiar two-finger Hook 'em Horns, the Texas players held up three fingers for the third year in a row Texas had found a way to win—and OU, a way to lose.

CARL MAYES

Not long after World War II, Bud Wilkinson's Sooners rolled to one of the greatest runs in college football history. After winning 31 consecutive games, Oklahoma followed up with 47 straight—the longest winning streak in the history of college football. But in between the two winning streaks, the Longhorns managed to squeeze in a victory. And did so without their star player.

After winning the national title the year before, Wilkinson's Sooners saturated the headlines heading into the 1951 season. OU had a fabulous line with tackle Jim Weatherall, who would win the Outland Trophy that season, and guard J.D. Roberts, who would win it two years later. The star of the show, though,

was halfback Billy Vessels, who many projected to be a serious contender for the Heisman Trophy. But as they looked ahead to Texas, the Sooners stumbled against Texas A&M the second week of the season.

Texas, meanwhile, had a fine team under Ed Price, who had replaced Blair Cherry as coach. Cherry had faced pressure to resign after losing three straight to the Sooners. Behind halfback Gib Dawson, Texas made a rapid ascent up the polls to begin the season. The Steers stunned Bear Bryant's Kentucky Wildcats, who had upset the national champion Sooners, and snapped the 31-game winning streak in the Sugar Bowl the year before. Texas then hammered Purdue and North Carolina, and suddenly was ranked sixth in the country. "I can't see how we can win this week when Texas has a better team than Texas A&M," Wilkinson said the week of the game. Of course, that was predicated on the Horns having Dawson in the lineup.

The morning of the game, the Longhorns were prepping to depart the Dallas Melrose Hotel. Five minutes before they were scheduled to board the bus, Dawson's father, only 40 years old, collapsed in the lobby of the hotel as he wished his son good luck in the game. Moments later, he died before the entire team.

Three years before, the Sooners had experienced a similar tragedy. The night before their game at Kansas, a late-night, long-distance telephone call notified Merle Greathouse that his mother had died of a heart ailment. Greathouse cried through the night with roommate Darrell Royal, but decided to play the next day. Dawson, who was in shock, was unable to.

TEXAS' ALL-TIME RED RIVER RIVALRY TEAM

OFFENSE

QB Peter Gardere (1989–1992): Gardere is the only Texas QB to beat OU four times.

RB Ricky Williams (1995–1998): The Heisman winner rolled over OU for 362 yards in '97 and '98 wins.

RB Earl Campbell (1974–1977): Barry Switzer called the Heisman winner the best player he faced in the series.

WR Cotton Speyrer (1968–1970): Speyrer led Texas rally in '69 with a record 160 receiving yards.

WR Johnny Walker (1987–1990): Walker hauled in the 25-yard game-winning touchdown from Peter Gardere in '89.

TE Bob Bryant (1956–1958): Bryant snapped OU's six-game winning streak with a game-winning touchdown catch in '58.

OT Justin Blalock (2003–2006): A two-time All-American, Blalock paved the way for Texas routs in '05 and '06.

OT Jerry Sisemore (1970–1972): Behind Sisemore, Texas' wishbone rushed for 310 yards and scored 41 points in the '70 rout.

OG Harley Sewell (1950–1952): The two-way star keyed Texas to victory in '51.

OG Johnny Treadwell (1960–1962): Treadwell, a unanimous All-American in '62, went 3–0 against Bud Wilkinson.

C Forrest Wiegand (1967–1969): Wiegand, a key cog in the Texas wishbone, never lost to the Sooners.

DEFENSE

DE Brian Orakpo (2005–2008) Orakpo sacked Sam Bradford twice in '08.

DT Stonie Clark (1992–1995): Clark stuffed James Allen at goal line in Texas '94 victory.

DT Scott Appleton (1961–1963): Appleton destroyed OU's offensive line with 18 tackles and a fumble recovery in '63.

DE Shane Dronett (1989–1991): Dronett totaled 21 total tackles in '90 and '91.

LB Tommy Nobis (1963–1965): Nobis had 21 tackles in '64, and had picks in '63 and '65—all Texas wins.

LB Jeff Lieding (1980–1983) Lieding racked up double-digit tackles in '81, '82, and '83.

LB Scott Henderson (1968–1970) Henderson finished with 18 tackles as UT beat Steve Owens in '69.

DB Stanley Richard (1987–1990): Richard finished with 32 career tackles against the Sooners.

DB Bryant Westbrook (1993–1996): Westbrook forced four turnovers alone in Texas' win in '94.

DB Johnnie Johnson (1976–1979): Johnson made the fourth-down stop on OU quarterback Thomas Lott to seal Texas' 1977 win.

DB Earl Thomas (2007–2009): Thomas picked off three passes in the Horns' 2008 and '09 wins.

SPECIAL TEAMS

K Russell Erxleben (1975–1978): In '77 Erxleben nailed field goals of 64 and 58 yards, the two longest in the series.

P Ernie Koy (1962–1965): The Texas halfback bottled up the Sooners with his punts in '62.

KR Jordan Shipley (2007–2010): Shipley's touchdown return in '08 spearheaded Texas' rally.

PR Bohn Hilliard (1932–1934): Hilliard 95-yard touchdown return remains a school record.

T E X A S

To replace his leading rusher and scorer, Price called on Carl Mayes. Nicknamed "Red," Mayes had never even lettered and had carried the ball only 10 times the season before. He would earn his letter this day.

Texas jumped on the board with a quick safety, then a Sooners fumble handed the Horns the ball deep in OU territory. Mayes made them pay, with a one-yard touchdown over left guard to give the Horns an early 9–0 lead. That proved to be enough.

In the fourth quarter, Vessels took a pitch in the OU end zone and weaved through a couple of UT defenders to avoid another safety. But along the way, he was leveled by safety Don Cunningham. Vessels had to be carried off the field with a knee injury that would sideline him the rest of the season. The Sooners offense sputtered the rest of the way, and Mayes made a couple of key runs to seal the victory. Mayes outplayed Vessels—who would come back to win the Heisman the following season—and rushed for a game-high 102 yards on 15 carries.

The following week, Mayes—who would become a lingerie salesman after college—returned to a reserve role behind Dawson. It would be seven years before Texas would defeat the Sooners again.

4

GAMES OUR ANCESTORS HATED

1901: TEXAS 12, OKLAHOMA 6

Seven years before Oklahoma Territory became a state in the union, the universities of Oklahoma and Texas began settling their differences on the gridiron. In the fall of 1895, Oklahoma organized its first football team under student Jack Harts. One day, while getting his hair trimmed in Bud Risinger's barbershop, Harts declared it was time for the school to put together a squad. Harts' footballers played one game that season against an opponent from Oklahoma City comprised of high school and college students from the Methodist College. Harts' boys were drubbed 34–0.

Five years later in 1900, Oklahoma played its first game against Texas and was whupped there, too, 28–2. But by 1901, with four years under the tutelage of coach V.L. Parrington, the Oklahoma Rough Riders started to become competitive.

In the 1901 season, Oklahoma scheduled two games with Texas, the first in Austin, the second in Norman. For the first game, the Oklahoma team traveled to Texas in the luxury of

Pullman cars. Playing with horse collars as shoulder pads, the Rough Riders had the mighty Steers on the ropes. Behind the hard running of their coach and halfback, Fred Roberts, who wore a blue jersey, the Sooners matched Texas play for play. After Sam Leslie scored to give the Steers a 6–0 lead just before half, OU countered with its first-ever touchdown in the series, courtesy of Tom Tribbey. But with 56 seconds left in the game, Texas' Bill McMahon swept around the end, then stiff-armed an OU safety on his way to the game-winning touchdown. The second meeting between the two schools wasn't as close. In front of a Norman crowd of 1,200, Texas prevailed again, 11–0.

1903: TEXAS 11, OKLAHOMA 5

Think losing on a Statue of Liberty play is gut-wrenching? Try losing on a fumble recovery under a horse.

Again in 1903, OU and Texas played a home-and-home. After the first game in Austin resulted in a 6–6 tie, the Longhorns returned the trip in Oklahoma City at Colcord Park a month later. There, the Longhorns scored on one of the oddest touchdowns in college football history. From the OU 25-yard line, Texas lined up to punt. Back then, the rules stated if a punt traveled past the goal line and off the playing field, it could still be recovered either for a touchdown or a touchback. Bill "Mogul" Robinson's punt ventured through the field of play into a group of horse-drawn coaches. Robinson and OU's Byrom McCreary dashed for the loose ball, which had rolled under a horse hitched to a buggy. McCreary sprinted to the other side of the horse, but Robinson dove head first under the horse's belly and recovered the ball for a touchdown. Texas won 11–5.

1906: TEXAS 10, OKLAHOMA 9

One year after beating Texas for the first time, coach Bennie Owen and Oklahoma welcomed the Longhorns back to Oklahoma City in front of 5,000 fans. But again, a change to the rulebook doomed the Boomers.

OU led late in the game, 9–4, thanks to Vernon Walling, a freshman from Tonkawa who set up OU's field goal and touchdown with fumble-causing tackles on Texas punt returns. But the Longhorns scored due to a new (and now defunct) rule— the onside punt, in which any punt past the line of scrimmage could be recovered by the kicking team as soon as it touched the ground.

After faking a run, reserve Ballard Coldwell reared back and boomed a punt down the sideline. Teammate Henry Fink scooped it up and stepped across the goal line for the touchdown, and Winston McMahon's extra point gave Texas the win. The Boomers couldn't complain too much. They scored their only touchdown on a similar play earlier in the game. It was also a valiant effort by Owen's squad, considering two of

TIES *IN THE* SERIES

1903: OU 6, Texas 6
1937: OU 7, Texas 7
1976: (No. 3) OU 6, (No. 16) Texas 6
1984: (No. 3) OU 15, (No. 1) Texas 15
1995: (No. 13) OU 24, (No. 18) Texas 24

TEXAS

its best players, halfbacks Harry Hughes and Owen Acton, were sidelined most of the day with charley horses.

The next day, the *Daily Oklahoman* reported, "Texas beef and brawn, pitted against Oklahoma pluck and courage, won for the University of Texas 11."

1929: TEXAS 21, OKLAHOMA 0

First, OU was shut out by Texas. Then, the stock market crashed, and Oklahoma, with the rest of the country, spiraled into the Great Depression. That, the ensuing Dust Bowl, and John Steinbeck's *The Grapes of Wrath* severely tainted Oklahoma's national reputation, which Sooners football ultimately helped repair.

Neither OU nor Texas had particularly strong teams in 1929, but that didn't stop the Texas State Fair from selling 2,500 standing-room-only tickets. After a scoreless first half, Texas captain Dexter Shelley recovered a Frank Crider fumble in Sooners territory. Shelley later plunged into the end zone to put Texas ahead 7–0. After the first quarter, the Sooners managed to gain only three first downs, and the Longhorns punched in two more touchdowns, one coming after OU fumbled inside its own 5-yard line.

The game was played under an overcast sky, which only became drearier for the Sooners faithful. But they had no idea how dreary life would get. The game was played on October 19, 1929, as the stock market was crumbling. By Monday, panic had taken hold. By Thursday, the market began to plunge. And then on October 29—Black Tuesday—the market crashed.

1940: TEXAS 19, OKLAHOMA 16

In its storied tradition, Oklahoma has had few notable collapses. But on October 12, 1940, the Sooners suffered one of their worst. Spearheaded by "Indian" Jack Jacobs, OU led Texas 16–13 and had the ball with only five minutes to go.

On third down, OU lined up in punt formation to try and pin the Longhorns deep and give its defense a chance to close out the game. But center Cliff Speegle's snap sailed over Jacobs' head, sending Jacobs after the ball to fall on it. Despite the gaffe, the Sooners still had another down to punt the ball. But overcompensating, Speegle kept the ball too low, skipping it along the ground. The poor back-to-back snaps gave Texas the ball at the OU 18-yard line. With three minutes to play, Texas tailback Jack Crain swept around the right end behind several "thudding blocks" for the nine-yard, game-winning score, his third touchdown of the day.

Speegle couldn't bring himself to watch that play. After the second bad snap, he hobbled off the field with his head lowered, then broke down behind the Sooners bench and began to weep. Several of his teammates went over and did their best to console him.

"Cliff Speegle, University of Oklahoma senior center and as fine a young man as ever struck his head through a pair of shoulder pads, left this field with a broken heart Saturday night," reported the *Daily Oklahoman's* Bus Ham. "Cliff felt personally responsible for Oklahoma's defeat by the University of Texas, 19 to 16, in a game that kept the 33,000 spectators perspiring not only from the heat but also from the jitters."

TEXAS

TEXAS WINS OVER THE SOONERS

1900: OU 2, Texas 28

1901: OU 6, Texas 12

1901: OU 0, Texas 11

1902: OU 6, Texas 22

1903: OU 5, Texas 11

1904: OU 10, Texas 40

1906: OU 9, Texas 10

1907: OU 10, Texas 29

1909: OU 0, Texas 30

1913: OU 6, Texas 14

1914: OU 7, Texas 32

1916: OU 7, Texas 21

1922: OU 7, Texas 32

1923: OU 14, Texas 26

1929: OU 0, Texas 21

1930: OU 7, Texas 17

1931: OU 0, Texas 3

1932: OU 10, Texas 17

1934: OU 0, Texas 19

1935: OU 7, Texas 12

1936: OU 0, Texas 6

1940: OU 16, Texas 19

1941: OU 7, Texas 40

1942: OU 0, Texas 7

1943: OU 7, Texas 13

1944: OU 0, Texas 20

1945: OU 7, No. 10 Texas 12

1946: OU 13, No. 1 Texas 20

1947: No. 15 OU 14, No. 3 Texas 34

1951: No. 11 OU 7, No. 6 Texas 9

1958: No. 2 OU 14, No. 16 Texas 15

1959: No. 13 OU 12, No. 4 Texas 19

1960: OU 0, No. 15 Texas 24

1961: OU 7, No. 4 Texas 28

1962: OU 6, No. 2 Texas 9

1963: No. 1 OU 7, No. 2 Texas 28

1964: OU 7, No. 1 Texas 28

1965: OU 0, No. 1 Texas 19

1967: OU 7, Texas 9

1968: OU 20, Texas 26

1969: No. 8 OU 17, No. 2 Texas 27

1970: OU 9, No. 2 Texas 41

1977: No. 2 OU 6, No. 5 Texas 13

1979: No. 3 OU 7, No. 4 Texas 16

1980: No. 12 OU 13, No. 3 Texas 20

1981: No. 10 OU 14, No. 3 Texas 34

1983: No. 8 OU 16, No. 2 Texas 28

1989: No. 15 OU 24, Texas 28

1990: No. 4 OU 13, Texas 14

1991: No. 6 OU 7, Texas 10

1992: No. 16 OU 24, Texas 34

1994: No. 16 OU 10, No. 15 Texas 17

1997: OU 24, Texas 27

1998: OU 3, Texas 34

1999: OU 28, No. 23 Texas 38

2005: OU 12, No. 2 Texas 45

2006: No. 14 OU 10, No. 7 Texas 28

2008: No. 1 OU 35, No. 5 Texas 45

2009: No. 20 OU 13, No. 3 Texas 16

The victory launched an eight-game series winning streak for the Longhorns, which remains the second-longest in OU-Texas history. Speegle, however, eventually recovered and ultimately stayed in football. He went on to become the head coach at Oklahoma State in 1955 and coached OSU to the 1958 Bluegrass Bowl, the school's only bowl appearance between 1948 and 1974. He also became the commissioner of the Southwest Conference in 1973.

5
TRADITIONS WE HATE

BEVO

Bevo. It's what's for dinner. As a matter of fact, in 1920, it was. Texas' bovine mascot has a rather sordid past, beginning with how it got its name. UT historians dispute it, but Bevo's name is believed to have stemmed from a defeat to the Texas Aggies. According to legend, on February 12, 1917, a group of Aggies pranksters traveled to Austin in the dark of night and branded "13–0"—the score of A&M's win the previous year—on the side of the Texas steer, who then was known as "Bo." Embarrassed, Texas undergrads turned the *13* to a *B*, the dash to an *E*, then inserted a *V* before the *0*. From then on, the mascot was referred to as "Bevo."

Jim Nicar, director of the UT Heritage Society in Austin, claims the story is false. "While the first Bevo was indeed branded '13–0,' the rest of the tale isn't true," Nicar wrote. "Bevo acquired his name months before the Aggies paid their infamous visit, and the brand itself was never changed."

Instead, Nicar charges that the school's campus magazine, the *Alclade*, first named the animal "Bevo" in December 1916, and that the Longhorns never rebranded the animal to save face.

Bevo, the University of Texas mascot, stands in the north end zone before the start of the 2006 Texas-Oklahoma game at the Cotton Bowl.

The Aggies have not taken that claim without a fight. The following editorial appeared in the *Battalion*, the A&M student newspaper, in 2004, shortly after Nicar's arguments surfaced: "Denial is something they must teach Longhorns at Camp Texas, or maybe it's ingrained into Austinites.... Longhorns can conjure up all the best stories about Bevo's name coming from a popular beverage or from a news writer's article, but face the facts: we branded a '13–0' on the side of your precious pet steer, and you had to come up with a creative way to make it go away."

TEXAS

WHAT I *LOVE* ABOUT THE SOONERS

Because game days have become a family event with no awkward discussions. We save that for Christmas.

WHAT I *HATE* ABOUT THE LONGHORNS

I grew to loathe Texas truly after the 2009 game. Texas fans cheered when Bradford went down with injury.

—*Jess Stiver, Dewar, Oklahoma*

Subsequent Bevos have also been enveloped in controversy. Bevo II once charged a SMU cheerleader, who had to defend himself with his megaphone (UT claims the cheerleader attacked first). Bevo III escaped from his enclosure and ran wild across campus for two days, before he was lassoed. Bevo IV once broke free and scattered the Baylor band in 1949 before ramming into a parked car.

Perhaps they deserved the same fate as Bevo I. In 1920 the UT administration grew tired of shelling out the 50¢ a day to feed the steer. So they shipped Bevo to a slaughterhouse, after which he was barbecued and served to the players at a Texas football banquet.

HOOK 'EM, HORNS

In Oklahoma, it's more acceptable to give the middle finger than the "Hook 'em Horns." The middle finger might get you a dirty look. The "Hook 'em Horns" might get you punched, or worse.

Roots of the hand signal go back to a 1955 pep rally, when UT male cheerleader Harley Clark taught the students a gesture to counter Texas A&M's "Gig 'em" sign. Fellow student Henry Pitts had actually invented the signal and had shown Clark how to do it. "A lot of my friends thought it would be too corny," Clark would later say. "But I thought it was perfect." Maybe Clark should have listened to his friends.

Texas head coach Mack Brown and players give the Hook 'em Horns after beating No. 1 Oklahoma 45–35 in 2008.

TEXAS

WHAT I *LOVE* ABOUT THE SOONERS

Family and tradition. My grandfather was a Sooners fan, and my daughter screams out, "Boomer Sooner!" every time she sees the OU logo.

WHAT I *HATE* ABOUT THE LONGHORNS

Growing up in Austin, you can't go two seconds without hearing a Texas fan saying they're God's gift to football, but we know who has the most trophies.

—*Dustin Shutack, Austin, Texas*

The "Hook 'em Horns" didn't exactly translate to success on the field. The day after the pep rally, TCU routed the Longhorns 47–20. "TCU had a fine team," Clark would say. "We had to make up in spirit what we lacked on the football field."

Two decades later, *Sports Illustrated* featured the "Hook 'em Horns" symbol in front of a Texas pennant on the cover of its September 10, 1973, issue, which argued that the Longhorns had the best program in college football. A month later, Texas was edged out by the Sooners 52–13.

BURNT ORANGE

Texas baseball might have the best sports tradition in Austin. It's also mostly responsible for UT's burnt orange and white colors.

According to school historians, UT founded a baseball team in 1885 and began playing other teams around the state. As a

chartered train was about to head north so Texas could take on Southwestern University in Georgetown, a pair of coeds declared they needed ribbon to identify themselves as Texas supporters. Their dates jumped off the train and went to the closest general store and asked for two colors of ribbon.

"What colors?" the shopkeeper asked. "Anything," the boys replied. So the shopkeeper handed them white, which he had plenty of because of weddings, and bright orange, because, well, nobody else ever bought that color. On the train ride to Georgetown, the ribbon was distributed to everyone on board, and bright orange and white became UT's unofficial colors.

For three decades, the Texas football team wore bright orange on their uniforms. But after several washes, the colors faded to

WHAT I LOVE ABOUT THE SOONERS

Bud Wilkinson's 47-game winning streak. I grew up in Ponca City, and dad took me to see OU when I was 'bout five. It was like a trip to heaven. I fell in love sitting on dad's shoulders, and 54 years later it is my longest and most cherished relationship. They have broken my heart many times, but the times they have given bliss far outweigh the bad times.

WHAT I HATE ABOUT THE LONGHORNS

It took a long time to develop a healthy hate. When I lived in Texas, they always sported that ugly orange, and constantly were bragging and putting OU down. I learned to hate them and never looked back. They earned it.

—*Charley Ashton, Nashville, Tennessee*

TEXAS

WHAT I **LOVE** ABOUT THE SOONERS

I spent seven wonderful years growing up at the University of Oklahoma, undergrad and graduate. I was there in the '70s and couldn't decide whether I wanted to be a hippie or a sorority princess. I tried both and finally settled on just being me, somewhere in the wonderful Oklahoma middle. Even today, "Boomer Sooner" gives me chills and the "OU Chant" brings happy tears.

WHAT I **HATE** ABOUT THE LONGHORNS

In the '70s driving through Austin on the way to visit my boyfriend, I was stopped by a Texas Ranger on I-35 right in front of Texas' football stadium. He asked if I was an OU student (I was wearing an OU T-shirt). He didn't even listen to my pleas as he wrote me a big fat ticket and snickered all the way back to his car. Still makes me mad 40 years later.

—*Sherri Boyd, Oklahoma City*

yellow by the end of the season, prompting opponents to refer to the Longhorns as "yellow bellies." In 1928 football coach Clyde Littlefield ordered uniforms in a darker shade of orange that wouldn't fade. Otherwise known as burnt orange.

BIG BERTHA

Texas proclaims "Big Bertha" to be the world's largest drum, with a diameter of eight feet and a width of 44 inches. Of course, this proclamation is subjective. Just ask Purdue.

"Big Bertha" was actually a reclamation project via the University of Chicago. After seeing the size of Purdue's drum during a 1921 football game, Chicago boosters demanded their

school build a similar drum. The next year, Chicago had its drum, which was taller than Purdue's, but skinnier.

The Boilermakers thought the battle of the drums was over when Chicago later dropped its football program and placed its drum in storage under the stands at Stagg Field, where scientists later actually would perform some of mankind's first nuclear experiments.

But in the 1950s the Chicago drum was sold to Dallas oil man Harold Byrd, who had it decontaminated and restored before giving it to the Longhorn Band. The battle of the drums was back on. In 1961 members of the band fraternity Kappa Kappa Psi at Purdue challenged their counterparts at Texas to a drum showdown at the fraternity's national convention in Wichita, Kansas.

Purdue showed up with their drum. The Longhorns did not. The Boilermakers claimed victory and have kept the dimensions of their drum a secret ever since. The only claim the Longhorns should be able to make is they own the "world's second-largest drum."

"THE EYES OF TEXAS"

"The Eyes of Texas" was written in 1903 by John Sinclair, who fitted the tune to, you guessed it, "I've Been Working on the Railroad." Sinclair, who penned the lyrics for a minstrel show performance, actually was poking fun at UT president Colonel William Prather. Prather had graduated from Washington College (now Washington and Lee University), whose president, Robert E. Lee, frequently reminded his

TEXAS

THE LYRICS TO "THE EYES OF TEXAS"

The Eyes of Texas are upon you,
All the live long day.
The Eyes of Texas are upon you,
You cannot get away.

Do not think you can escape them
At night or early in the morn—
The Eyes of Texas are upon you
'Til Gabriel blows his horn.

students that "the eyes of the South are upon you." Prather and Lee became close. In fact, Prather was a pallbearer at Lee's funeral in 1870.

Lee's phrase stuck with Prather, who always ended his speeches as UT's president with, "The eyes of Texas are upon you," setting the inspiration for Sinclair's tune. Before long, the song became the school's official alma mater.

TEXAS FIGHT

Usually following "The Eyes of Texas" is "Texas Fight," the official fight song of the Longhorns. Colonel Walter S. Hunnicutt wrote the song in collaboration with James E. King. Hunnicutt said he wrote the song because the Texas Aggies were ridiculing "The Eyes of Texas," presumably for its painful adagio, during football games. The first strain of "Texas Fight" is actually a sped-up of version of "Taps," the trumpet solo played at military funerals

THE LYRICS *TO* "TEXAS FIGHT"

Texas fight, Texas fight,
And it's good-bye to A&M.
Texas fight, Texas fight,
And we'll put over one more win.
Texas fight, Texas fight,
For it's Texas that we love best.
Give 'em hell, give 'em hell, go, Horns, go!
And it's good-bye to all the rest!

(YELL)
Yea orange! Yea white!
Yea Longhorns! Fight! Fight! Fight!
Texas fight! Texas fight!
Yea Texas fight!
Texas fight! Texas fight!
Yea Texas fight!

TEXAS

In the Red River game, UT fans sub out the line "Give 'em hell, give 'em hell, go, Horns, go!" with "Give 'em hell, give 'em hell, OU sucks!"

"Texas Fight" is usually reserved for after touchdowns, meaning the Longhorn Band got to boom it all of twice in the Cotton Bowl in 2011.

SMOKEY THE CANNON

In 1953 "Smokey the Cannon" was commissioned for construction by UT's engineering department. The impetus for the cannon's creation was for the Longhorns to have some

TEXAS

WHAT I *LOVE* ABOUT THE SOONERS

The tradition of a powerhouse program; coaches like Wilkinson, Switzer, Stoops; players like Steve Owens, the Selmon brothers, Billy Sims, Brian Bosworth, Jason White, Derrick Strait, Tommie Harris, Sam Bradford, Rocky Calmus, Roy Williams, Adrian Peterson, Jermaine Gresham, Ryan Broyles; seven national titles; the longest winning streak in college football.

WHAT I *HATE* ABOUT THE LONGHORNS

They get a lot of attention, but are vastly overrated. They get these highly ranked recruiting classes but underachieve and don't develop their players. If OU had the resources and facilities that Texas has, there would be no rivalry.

—Anthony Ganey, Tallahassee, Florida

celebratory firepower, a direct response to the shotgun blasts of OU's RUF/NEKS after Sooners scores.

Texas probably should have focused on building a better football team. In Smokey's debut, OU prevailed 19–14 in what would be the second of six consecutive wins over the Longhorns. Later that year, "Smokey I" met its demise, although there are two versions to that story. The first is that some enterprising Texas Aggies stole the cannon and tossed it into Lake Austin. The other version was that Smokey malfunctioned or was knocked over, causing it to sling an exploding firework between the speaker of the Texas House of Representatives and his pregnant wife.

Whatever the case, UT sent the cannon back to the School of Engineering for renovation. The cannon returned in 1955, but was essentially left uncorked in the Cotton Bowl. The Longhorns failed to reach the end zone once, as OU blanked them 20–0.

The third and current cannon, "Smokey III," a Civil War replica, replaced "Smokey II" in 1989 and shoots five blank, 10-gauge shotgun shells. It costs roughly $8 every time it's

WHAT I *LOVE* ABOUT THE SOONERS

As most Oklahomans, I was born into the OU fan base with my dad being a huge OU fan. We used to watch every game that was on TV and listen to the rest on the radio. We never really got to go to the games, so when I was in medical school, I got my own tickets, and now I haven't missed an OU-Texas game in over 20 years. It's always the most exciting trip of the year.

WHAT I *HATE* ABOUT THE LONGHORNS

I used to think that everyone had a few bad fans that ruined it for everyone else. But Texas has the worst. Even after the beatdowns, they act like it was just a fluke and that their dominance is still overwhelming and that the next year will be theirs. But the true reason I hate Texas is from an incident when I took my 10-year old son to the game. Texas had won, and my son was carrying a stuffed animal he'd won playing a game, and a 40-year-old Texas fan jumped in front of him and yelled, "Well, at least you OU fans can win at something!" Texas fans have no class.

—*Dr. Shawn Clinton Schlinke, Oklahoma City*

TEXAS

fired, meaning Texas left the Cotton Bowl last year with a rather small bill.

TORCHLIGHT PARADE

It's amazing the Torchlight Parade survived. Originally a parade saved for the night before UT's game against Texas A&M, the Torchlight Parade went dormant in the 1960s. It was rebooted in 1987 as part of the OU-Texas week. Days after the Torchlight Parade was revived, Barry Switzer's Sooners stomped out Texas 44–9 in one of the biggest routs in the history of the series, OU's third straight win over Texas.

WHAT I *LOVE* ABOUT THE SOONERS

The successful and enduring tradition of OU football sums up my loyalty to the program. Through the years OU football players learn about pride in their work and the work ethic required to be successful. OU football leadership stresses core values like team, unity and loyalty. These values are manifested on the field of competition and through the years have produced championship football at a high level of play. Coaches, players, and fans all expect a high level of play every year based on the successful formula of OU football and its rich tradition.

WHAT I *HATE* ABOUT THE LONGHORNS

The long tradition of this heated rivalry is not only entertaining but engaging. You can't stand on the sidelines of this game without taking a side. I remember my first OU-Texas game and feeling the electricity in the air when the Longhorns fans started their "Texas Fight" chant. I knew what side I was on and always would be. Boomer Sooner, baby.

—*Jeff Myers, Santa Ana, California*

TEXAS

WHAT I *LOVE* ABOUT THE SOONERS

When I was a kid, before every game was televised, fall Saturdays were about tuning to KRMG to hear John Brooks and Mike Treps bring us OU football action. It was our team, Barry's boys, going out and stamping "Oklahoma" on campuses across the country and on the field at the Orange Bowl. I am proud that my state's university is home to the No. 1 football program of the modern era. I am proud that Bob's boys are doing the same and continuing the tradition.

WHAT I *HATE* ABOUT THE LONGHORNS

Hate is a strong word, but generally Texas stands between OU and a championship. The success of one team's season is often inversely proportional to that of the other's. Texans look down their noses at us and the rest of the country. Former Sooners tight end Trent Smith may have summed it best: "Burnt orange makes me puke."

—Jay Kelley, Oaks, Oklahoma

The Longhorns, however, hung on to the tradition, and every year, they march around Austin before arriving at the University of Texas Tower for the "Beat OU" rally. Since reinstituting the Torchlight Parade, Texas has lost 12 times to the Sooners, and counting.

UT TOWER

Tragically, the University of Texas Tower is synonymous with one of the deadliest shootings in American history. On August 1, 1966, student Charles Whitman perched on top of the tower with a sniper rifle and killed 16 people while wounding 32 others.

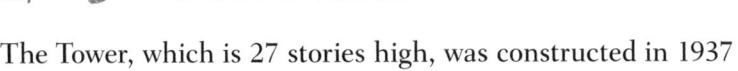

The Tower, which is 27 stories high, was constructed in 1937 and features a sophisticated lighting system used to commemorate different events at the university.

The Tower glows entirely in orange after Texas victories over the Sooners. Suffice to say the Tower was rarely orange in October from 2000 to 2004.

The UT Tower lighting guidelines:

- Entirely white: standard
- White top with orange shaft: academic achievements
- Orange top with white shaft: football victories
- Entirely orange: significant football victories, including OU, Texas A&M, and conference championships; also commencement, Texas Independence Day, and the school's birthday
- Orange with white No. 1: national championships in any sport
- Darkened with white top: solemn occasions
- Top split orange and white with orange shaft: welcoming new students to campus

HOOK 'EM

A cursory glance at "Hook 'em," the Longhorns' goofball costumed mascot, has been known to instantly instill confidence in Texas' opponents.

"Hook 'em" actually got suspended from an Austin Super Regional after getting into an altercation with a fan during Texas' baseball game with Arizona State.

SOURCES

Books

Cross, George Lynn. *Presidents Can't Punt*. Norman: University of Oklahoma Press, 1977.

Dent, Jim. *The Undefeated*. New York: St. Martin's Press, 2002.

Dozier, Ray. *The Oklahoma Football Encyclopedia*. Champaign, IL: Sports Publishing, 2006.

Heard, Robert. *Oklahoma vs. Texas: When Football Becomes War*. Austin, TX: Honey Hill Publishing, 1980.

Keith, Harold. *Forty-Seven Straight: The Wilkinson Era at Oklahoma*. Norman: University of Oklahoma Press, 1984.

Shropshire, Mike. *Runnin' with the Big Dogs: The Long, Twisted History of the Texas-OU Rivalry*. New York: HarperCollins Publishers, 2006.

Wilkinson, Jay. *Bud Wilkinson: An Intimate Portrait of an American Legend*. Champaign, IL: Sagamore Publishing, 1994.

Other Sources

Associated Press
Austin American-Statesman
Daily Oklahoman
Dallas Morning News
Dallas Times Herald
Fort Worth Star-Telegram
Houston Chronicle
Norman Transcript
Sports Illustrated Vault
Tulsa World
University of Oklahoma Sports Information Department Archives